This guide should app
It should also be of in
of the natural environ

There are some nice, easy walks which can be taken at leisure at an easy pace.

There are also some more difficult ones which will appeal to the more energetic walker looking for a bit of adventure, some stretching of the limbs, and possibly a little intellectual and observational exercise in communion with nature.

The guide is written by an older walker and a much younger photographer.

It was compiled in the recognition that most of the guides – and there are not that many – were written for families to take gentle and sensible walks or rambles on fairly easy paths.

Some of these walks have been deliberately chosen to be more difficult, although it must be said that many of them are really quite a doddle.

There is a wealth of material on Gower covering natural history, folklore and so on, but no one walking guide which covers the whole coastline and which explains, however briefly, what to expect, and what to see on each walk.

It was for this purpose that this guide was written covering walks that can be completed in anything from one to five hours depending on the terrain, the weather, fitness and personal choice.

The one thing above all that the contributors hope to achieve is that readers will enjoy the walks, get some exercise benefits and will pass on some of their experiences so that many others will enjoy the unique and remarkable environment that is the Gower coastline the very one whose scenery resulted in the Gower peninsula being declared the United Kingdom's first Area of Outstanding Natural Beauty in 1956.

If you wish to take up the challenge, it will take several weeks of evening walks and a weekend or two to complete the series.

An alternative – and probably much more sensible way – is simply to pick off the walks one by one as the fancy takes you and maybe after a year or so find the series has been completed.

This book covers 16 coastal walks, a second series covering a further 12 walks will complete the series.

Contents

GRADING OF WALKS

1 Easy walking on generally well-marked and well-used paths or tracks.

2 A generally easy walk with a few rough patches and hilly sections.

3 Moderately difficult with a fair amount of climbing and several rough parts.

4 A tough walk with plenty of ups and downs, frequent rough patches and occasional dangerous stretches.

5 Difficult walk for serious and experienced walkers only, with stiff climbs and sheer cliff overhangs — challenging.

Note The less-experienced should not be deterred from the more difficult walks — just be more wary. In these circumstances, it may be wise to have company.
If a walker should decide to choose one of the alternative routes on a walk then the degree of difficulty may well rise. The guide to each walk contains a comment on its grading and suitability for children.

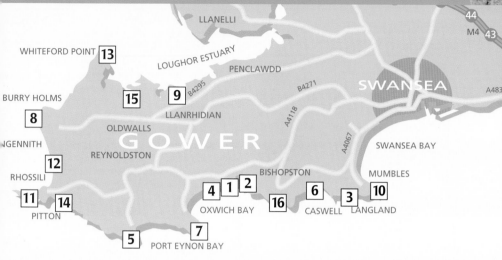

MAPS

- We urge the use of Ordnance Survey walkers' maps, available at outdoor pursuits stores and some bookshops.
- Map reference numbers appear in our walks, eg MR 527885.

KEY TO SYMBOLS

ℹ Information	⛫ Castle	⌂ Ancient remains
🅿 Parking	✝ Church	▲ Triagulation point
☀ View points	⬧ Farm	⊟ Refreshments

The walks marked with the National Trust (NT) logo include some or all of their length on NT land. The National Trust works to conserve the coast and countryside. It is a charity and owns 5,500 acres of Gower.

Biographies

The Walker
DR GORDON AVERY

TRAVEL STORIES - DR GORDON AVERY

Dr Avery is a public health physician. He recently spent two years (1998-2000) as Chief Medical Officer on Montserrat in the West Indies where he helped restore the health services following the major volcanic eruptions.

Dr Avery's earlier career was as a deck officer in the Merchant Navy. After medical studies he became a medical officer in the colonial medical service in the Solomon Islands, north east of Australia.

He was later the director of public health for South Warwickshire for 15 years. From 1995 to 1998 and again during 2001 he was a consultant in public health medicine with Iechyd Morgannwg Health (formerly West Glamorgan Health Authority) in Swansea. While there he helped to set up the South West Wales Cancer Institute and was its first director. In addition to his medical duties, Dr Avery took a keen interest in the Gower peninsula where he spent many summer evenings walking the coastal paths. He felt the need to record these walks and welcomed the opportunity to team up with photographer Louise Beddow to produce a series of guidance notes on the Gower Coastal Walks.

The Photographer
LOUISE BEDDOW

Louise is a freelance landscape and natural history photographer based in Llangennith on the Gower peninsula.

From an early age, Louise expressed a keen interest in the natural world and, after completing a BA (Hons) in film and photography, decided to establish herself documenting the flora, fauna and spectacular scenery of Gower. In her spare time, Louise enjoys backpacking and camping her way around the British Isles. A three-year field study of Sanday in the Orkney Islands resulted in an exhibition of work in Kirkwall and recent excursions have seen her explore the Scilly Isles, Skomer and Flatholm in west Wales, the west coast of Ireland, Ben Nevis, Glencoe and Skye. Her portfolio of work includes the building up of a photolibrary for the National Trust at Dynevor Park, Llandeilo. She produced

ONE WOMAN AND HER DOG - LOUISE BEDDOW AND TANSY.

a weekly infoburst on WatchOut, at Bristol's Natural History Unit and was a camerawoman on the six-part series Penclacwydd: Blwyddyn Gron, for Teledu Telesgop.

She has a CD Rom on display at Rhossili which shows multimedia interactive walks around Gower. Louise was delighted to produce this walks guide with Dr Avery, encouraging the enjoyment of Gower.

This guide is a revised and updated version of the South Wales Evening Post supplement first issued in 1998 and re-issued in December 2000 as the 'eagerly awaited reprint of a hugely popular publication'. The supplement was issued as part of the SWEP Cancer Fund. The authors are grateful to the SWEP for the opportunity to use original material and maps prepared by them for the supplement.

The natural history of Gower

WILD FOX ON GOWER

The main aspects of the natural history of Gower which are of interest to the walker are the birds and the wild flowers. The marine life will also be of interest, although with many of the paths being well above the seashore, this can often only be seen at a distance.

THE BIRDS

On all Gower walks, birds will be seen. The types will depend on the location the season and the weather but there will always be something. In contrast to the true birdwatcher who remains still and observant, the walker is likely to get only a fleeting glimpse of the birds.

He or she may even disturb birds from time to time. A few quiet moments, however, on a clifftop or by the side of a marsh may well bring rewards that the walker was not expecting.

It is important that the walker observes the Nature Conservancy Council signs at all times and doesn't disturb those sites which are particularly important during the breeding season from March 15. These include, most notably, the rocks and headlands of Thurba and the Outer Worm's Head.

FLOWER POWER - THE BLOODY CRANESBILL, A COLOURFUL SIGHT AT BROUGHTON.

The natural history of Gower

The best place to see the real seabirds — those that fish for a living — is anywhere along the south coast. The further west you go the better.
Good places are Burry Holms and Whiteford Point. Here you will see cormorants, shags and, occasionally, gannets flying by. There could also be razorbills and guillemots.

Waders and marsh birds may be seen, especially around Burry Pill and Whiteford Point as well as Oxwich Bay and Broughton. To recognise all the different types takes the eye of an expert but you will see rock pippits, turnstones, snipe, redshank, sandpipers, plovers, dunlins, curlews and oystercatchers. In the Loughor Estuary you will spot many wildfowl on their way to the Wetlands

Most likely are buzzards, kestrels and sparrowhawks. Occasionally peregrines and harriers may be spotted.

Other birds on clifftops include ravens, rooks, crows and jackdaws — and watch out for the distinctive chough with red beak and legs *(usually seen on the headlands between East Cliff at Pennard and Hunt's Bay).*

Kingfishers, grey wagtails and herons can sometimes be spotted by Gower's many rivers and streams. Keep an eye out for the more commonly-seen pigeons, swallows, swifts and sparrows, not forgetting seagulls of many varieties, fulmars and kittiwakes.

SEASCAPE WORM'S HEAD FROM THE TOWERING HEIGHTS OF RHOSSILI DOWN.

Centre at Penclacwydd — Brent geese, Canada geese, shell ducks, mallards, herons and egrets.

A phone call to the Wildfowl and Wetland Centre at Penclacwydd or the Royal Society for the Protection of Birds (see contacts on page 80) should keep you informed on what to look for. Birds of prey may be seen, particularly on the cliff edges of Rhossili Down and some other clifftops.

THE WILD FLOWERS

The wild flowers of Gower are a delight.
The botanical pundit may well look for varieties like the yellow witlow grass or Isle of Man cabbage which can be found in the dunes around Three Cliffs Bay.

For lesser mortals there is still much to be enjoyed.

GRAZING RIGHTS - WILD PONIES ON RHOSSILI DOWN.

ROCKY THREE - ONE OF GOWER'S FAMOUS NATURAL LANDMARKS — THREE CLIFFS BAY.

knapweed, red and white clover, field scabious, common birds foot trefoil, harebells and red and white campion.

On the moorlands and heathlands of Mumbles Head, Rhossili Down and Port Eynon Point you will find gorse and heather, bracken and thistles, common ragwort, knapweed, vipers bugloss, spring squill, foxglove and scarlet pimpernel.

On the coastal littorals and rock pavements, you will find the beautiful sea thrift and golden samphire.

The habitats range from limestone crags to coastal and rock pavements, to moorland and heathland, to sand dunes and mudflats, the rivers, ponds and lakes and the woodlands, hedgerows, grassland and roadside verges.

The crags and rockfaces boast the greater

The sand dunes and shingle beaches like those at Oxwich Bay, Whiteford Point and Three Cliffs Bay have a range of flowers adapted to the environment, including Portland spurge, sea rocket, sea holly, bloody cranesbill, biting stonecrop and evening primrose.

The natural history of Gower

If all this isn't enough we also have sea aster, sea lavender and the yellow flag iris adorning the mud flats and marshes. In the rivers and ponds there are water lilies and bulrushes. There are also 14 or so species of orchid on Gower.

THE MARINE ANIMALS

The remaining fauna on Gower is not without interest. If you spend time at the rockpools on the causeway of Worm's Head, you will see many limpets, barnacles and crabs. Be careful not to be caught by the tide. Along the more rugged coastal parts of Gower you may see a common seal or two – they are not that common but one place to see them is on the outer head of the Worm.

OTHER ANIMALS

The common adder is seen from time to time in the gorse and scrub areas. It is a shy animal and far more frightened of you than you should be of it.

It may be found basking on a rock on a hot day and it does bite, albeit rarely. If it should bite you, wrap something like a vest or shirt tightly around the affected part and go to casualty or the accident and emergency unit at Singleton or Morriston hospitals.

SURF AND TURF MUMBLES HEAD AND THE WATERS OF SWANSEA BAY FROM BLACKPILL.

Hedgerows and woodlands boast bluebells and wood garlic, ramsons, herb robert and tormentil and finally never forget the grasslands and roadside verges where you can find daffodils, thistles, shepherds purse, foxglove, rosebay willowherb, yarrow and nipplewort.
The relatively rare and majestic great mullein may also be spotted. Remember to take photographs or sketches if you want a reminder of these delightful flowers – never be tempted to pick them.

These bites are never fatal. The grass snake is common on Gower. This is harmless and can be found in similar areas of habitat to the adder.

One other interesting animal is the glowworm – this can be seen in hedgerows at night on a warm summer's evening. Look out for weasels, badgers, foxes and bats – all common in Gower.

KING OF THE CASTLE - GREAT TOR

DISTANCE	2.2MILES/3.5KM
TIME	2 HOURS
GRADING	2 - 3

OUTLINE An excellent, not too demanding walk, which can be made more energetic by taking one or more of many possible diversions. When the tide is out it is possible to walk on the beach around Great and Little Tors. There are a number of historical sites, some fine views and some impressive limestone formations. The more adventurous can tackle the mildly challenging climb up to the top of the outermost peak of Great Tor.

TRANSPORT

BUS From Swansea's Quadrant to Port Eynon. Alight at Penmaen Old Post Office MR 527885.

CAR Take the A4118 from Swansea to Penmaen. Look out for the postbox and phone box at the western end of the village.

PARKING Park in the small free public car park at MR 526885. If this is full there are other car parks on the side roads leading up to Cefn Bryn.

COLOURFULL - ROSEBAY WILLOWHERB CAN BE FOUND ALL OVER GOWER

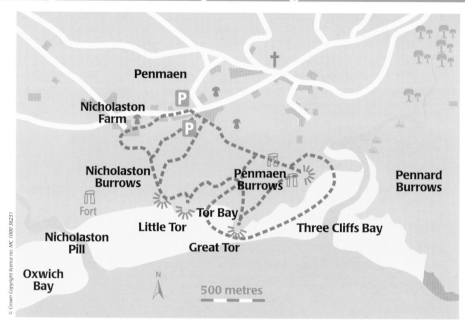

© Crown Copyright licence no. MC 1000 36231

WHERE TO START
At the car park in Penmaen.

PENMAEN TO THREE CLIFFS BAY LOOKOUT

From the car park go through the metal gate and take the prominent stony track in a south-easterly direction down towards Three Cliffs Bay. Keep on this track until you reach another metal gate, which opens on to the sandy dunes of Penmaen Burrows *(National Trust)*. Immediately to your right is a path which goes down to Tor Bay. Ignore this and keep going on the wide sandy path straight towards the clifftop overlooking Three Cliffs Bay *(you can divert to the left and go downhill to the bay and you can also divert to the right over the dunes to try to locate one of the ancient monuments)*.

The lookout gives you one of the best of all the views of Three Cliffs Bay with all its changing moods, depending on the weather and state of tide.

It is different every time you go there.

IMPRESSIVE SIGHT - THE BROAD SWEEP OF THREE CLIFFS BAY

WILD THING - THE COMMON TOADFLAX

CLIFFTOP WALK FROM THE LOOKOUT TO GREAT TOR

From the lookout head back to the main path then turn left and head south-west towards Great Tor.

This is a clear and undulating path through bracken.

Several diversions can be made towards the sea, each one leading to a rocky limestone spur with fine views out on to the Bristol Channel and along the coast.

In spring and summer there is a profusion of wild flowers on these mini headlands.

When you reach the final spur facing towards Great Tor you have a choice. The walk down the spur to the final rocky outcrop of Great Tor is more difficult than the cliff track.

It ends in a short, sharp, climb up to the tor which should *not be undertaken by the faint-hearted.* It is safe for the more adventurous and the skilled rock scrambler as long as great care is taken, especially on top of the tor. The reward, with its brilliant view over Oxwich and Three Cliffs Bay, is well worth the effort. Once on top you are truly the king of the castle.

Even more so than on the peak of Three Cliffs because you only occasionally meet people on top of Great Tor – and they are fellow enthusiasts anyway.

THE CLIMB UP GREAT TOR

Face towards the rocky outcrop. Climb up a small, well-worn chimney on to a ledge about 10ft above you. You can turn left and go up another gully another 10ft to 15ft to reach the top of the tor. An alternative from the first ledge is to face the sea and scramble up on to the sloping ledge above. Once there, you can turn right to go on to the lower of the two peaks.
By turning left and scrambling up a smooth sloping rock face *(with the seaward vertical slope on your right)* you can quickly and safely join the main peak.

the Penmaen Burrows and gradually work round to the top of the gully coming out of Tor Bay. There are a couple of benches here and, if you are already exhausted, you can turn right and head back across the dunes to rejoin the path you came down earlier. The more intrepid walkers will now continue along the good path above the bay. This passes a disused lime kiln and soon diverts out to the headland of Little Tor. This is worth the excursion but is nothing like as spectacular as Great Tor.
Once back on the path again you quickly reach a stile. By turning left here, in a matter of a few metres you are onto another small rocky outcrop, this time with a splendid view across Oxwich Bay and down onto Nicholaston Burrows.

GREAT TOR TO LITTLE TOR

From the top of the spur – whether or not you have completed the climb up Great Tor – head north on the prominent path on the edge of

PRETTY AS A PICTURE - A PEACOCK BUTTERFLY

LITTLE TOR TO PENMAEN

From the stile head north west on a winding and undulating path which skirts round the top of the burrows. There are several possibilities along this path both for turning inland and for going down onto the burrows or onto the extensive beach of Oxwich Bay.

Our route keeps along the top, walking through rough bush and bracken. It then enters woodland with the fields and caravans of Nicholaston Farm above you to the right.

Soon the path is joined by another path coming up from the left and then the main stepped path coming up from Nicholaston Burrows.

It quickly reaches the Nicholaston stream and gully *(often dry)* and heads up a short sharp flight of steps to join the farm track leading down from Nicholaston Farm. Go over the stone steps, up the road a few paces then turn right into Nicholaston Farm.

Dogs may bark here but they are used to visitors during the holiday season. Go through the double farm gates into a large concrete courtyard. Go past the farm buildings with a wall painting on your right: *"Enjoy the fruits of your labours"* and a sign saying: *"Children playing."*

Go through another gate into the caravan park and head diagonally uphill to your left. At the top north-east corner of the field there is a gate leading to a narrow path.

This soon turns to the left over a stile and goes between two dwellings direct to the main road. Turn right on the road head east and you are soon back to your starting point.

WHAT TO LOOK FOR

Geology Great Tor is a spur of vertical limestone strata.

Birds and other fauna Jackdaws, sanderling, pipits, robins. Many species of summer butterfly. Common lizard and goats.

History Sites of archaeological interest:

1 Penmaen megalithic tomb near Penmaen Old Castle, around 5,500 years old, large communal tomb;

2 Penmaen Old Castle, a stone bank fronted by a deep ditch on the cliff edge overlooking Three Cliffs, 12th Century Norman excavated in 1960;

3 Old Church, now just a stone walled depression in the dunes, this is where the first Penmaen church stood.

IN THE PINK - RED CAMPION

Botany Red campion, birds foot trefoil, red clover, common milkwort, ladys bedstraw, scabious, common toadflax, common dog violet

Conservation National Trust Land

Visual aspect Fantastic views of Oxwich Bay from the tors.

SLIPPERY CUSTOMER - A LIZARD

Penmaen to Three Cliffs

HIGH POINT - THREE CLIFFS

DISTANCE	2.5 MILES/4KM
TIME	2 - 3 HOURS
GRADING	2

OUTLINE Depending on the route you take, this is a relatively easy, enjoyable walk with long stretches of sandy beach. It has the advantage of a few rock climbs and dune scrambles if you wish to take them. From several places there are the most superb views of Three Cliffs Bay.

TRANSPORT

BUS From Swansea Quadrant to Port Eynon/Rhossili infrequently. Alight at bus stop at Penmaen Church. Note New round Gower service in summer.

CAR Take the A4118 out of Swansea to Parkmill then go up the hill until you see the sign "Penmaen". Once there turn right at the bus stop/phone/red post box leaving the small church on your left. Go 100m up the hill to the unmarked car park on a grassy area ahead of you at MR 532887 near to the National Trust Cefn Bryn sign.

PARKING This is forbidden (*double yellow lines*) on roads all around Penmaen and is unwise anyway. There are car parks at the western end of the village at MR 527886 and MR 526885. There is another small park up the lane from the church at MR 529887. This has a superb view of Oxwich and Three Cliffs bays but this is best reserved for people who want to come for the view. There is a famous view of Three Cliffs Bay from the main road at MR 530886.

COLOUR - BLOODY CRANESBILL

On a clear day you can see forever

WHERE TO START

The green by Penmaen Church opposite the bus stop MR 532887.

PENMAEN TO STREAM CROSSING

Face due east and cross the main road to the North Hills Lane *(not marked)*. Go along the lane leaving five houses/bungalows on your right and take the first road turning to the right *(there is a sign marked "Beach" on the far side)*.

Go downhill past a National Trust sign "Notthill" on the left then past some cottages as the road bears to the left and becomes rougher *(end of tarmac)*. Go past a small gate to the right *("Residents only – Stonesfield")* then reach a clear path going down to the right past a distinctive yellow emergency phone.

Your route from here will depend on the tide, which you are advised to check before starting.

Note the splendid views over the bays and the burrows.

If the tide is going out and not due to turn for an hour or so *(or even if it is just due to turn)* you may go straight down the steep stepped path from the main path at MR 534884.

This path goes past the Stonesfield shacks, turning gradually to the left at the bottom to open into the top tidal part of Penmaen Pill.

Here you will find another phone and a prominent warning sign *"Bathing in this area can be dangerous"*. From here you can go along the south side of the

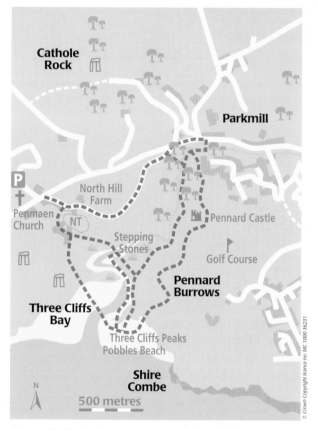

stream onto the beach or go over the slatted fenced path marked "National Trust Three Cliffs" – past another severe warning sign about bathing and down a small sandy slope onto the beach.

If the tide is rising rapidly or already in, then you will have to use the alternative route over the stepping stones – MR 538883 *(even these may be covered during exceptionally high tides in which case this particular route to the peaks is not open to you)*.

The route carries on steadily downhill from the yellow phone on a rough track until the tidal

margin is reached. A very short walk along the edge brings you to the stepping stones. A track continues here along the northern and western edge of Pennard Pill which eventually ends up at Parkmill. This is not recommended as it is exceedingly muddy in places and at high tide requires frequent diversions into thick, near impenetrable woodland.

Once over the stepping stones you can now cross over the shingle promontory then keep all the way on the north and east side of Pennard Pill to the Three Cliffs peaks.

SUN SPOT - THREE CLIFFS BAY

STREAM CROSSING TO THREE CLIFFS PEAKS — THE BEACH WALK

Once on the beach the choice is yours. If the tide is low you can go all the way on the beach round into Oxwich Bay. You can make straight for the Three Cliffs peaks but remember you will have to cross the swift-flowing Pennard Pill somewhere.

This is not usually a problem with waterproof walking boots or wellingtons — or you could choose to go barefoot.
Also remember to be quite sure about the tides and do not attempt to do this on a rising tide.

HOW TO CLIMB THE THREE PEAKS — NOT FOR THE FAINT-HEARTED

The Three Peaks increase in height from west to east.
The eastern-most highest peak is the easiest to climb. The other two are slightly more difficult. *Great care is needed at the top of all three.*

To climb the two lower peaks start at the western end of the group MR 538878.

Look for a natural gully going up the southern face and scramble up this, keeping the rock face to your left and generally some safe rock outcrops on your right. *(You will often see expert climbers on the slabs to your right and below you — they are very helpful if you need advice).* Keep on going up the gully until you reach the top of it, from which you can

only turn back and go up the eastern peak or go straight on diagonally up to the top of the middle peak.

Both of these peaks have a difficult — and potentially dangerous — last few feet. It is better if you have someone with you to complete these sections.

The highest peak is a doddle by comparison as long as you approach it from the eastern side. *(Do not attempt the climber's south side which looks easy but is actually difficult).* Start on the grassy slope at the bottom of the peak having arrived there either by a rock climb up from the Pobbles Bay or by coming along one of the paths off Pennard Burrows.

Go straight up, diagonally, in one of the series of natural rock steps.

Take a series of zig-zags to the top. It can be done in 60 seconds quite safely but take it easy on your first attempt. Keep generally on the seaward side but not too far over otherwise you are on to the expert climbers' slabs.

Do not go over the top because the other side is a sheer rock face. Once on top you are king of the castle.

You will have the most superb views of Three Cliffs Bay, Pennard Burrows, Pobbles Bay and all along the coastline to the east and west.

This is one of the best spots on Gower and is so easy to get to.

THE RETURN FROM THE THREE CLIFFS PEAKS TO PENMAEN

For your return to Penmaen you may go through the natural archway between the two eastern peaks and return along the eastern side of Pennard Pill to the stepping stones.

This is often wet and slippery — but not a bad walk.

It is possible — with some difficulty — to reach the dunes above from the stream but the cliffs there are deceptive and crumbly so be careful if you choose this route.

SAND BLASTED - PENNARD CASTLE

The other route goes up over the top of the dunes. There is a slightly difficult rock scramble up a ledge immediately to the east of the highest of the Three Cliffs peaks. This takes you to the base of the regular starting point for assaulting the peak at MR 539878.

An easier but slightly more tedious route is to go in at the Pobbles Beach inlet. Start walking up towards the golf clubhouse then divert off to the left on any one of the prominent footpaths. Try to find the "official" slatted path if you can.

It starts round about MR 541878. Somewhere from the highest part of the dunes you may then take one of the several paths back to the stepping stones. *(Some of these are periodically cordoned off for conservation purposes).*

Or you can keep on the slatted path over to Pennard Castle and on to Parkmill.

From the stepping stones go back up the gravel track, past the Stonesfield shacks and Notthill to Penmaen Church.

ALTERNATIVE ROUTES BACK TO PENMAEN

THE CRUMBLING CLIFFS WALK

The most interesting route to return starts at the base of the short climb up the eastern-most of the eastern Three Cliffs peaks MR 539878 and heads north west.

Then, turn north above the cliffs which overlook Pennard Pill as it comes round to the eastern edge of Three Cliffs Bay.

This is an undulating walk which is quite rocky in parts.

You need to be careful that you do not go off to the left on a "path of no return" which ends up overlooking an edge.

Equally, be wary when the path comes close to cliff overhangs as these can be crumbly. Better on this occasion to go up and over. This route finally ends up leading out to the shingle spur which juts out into Pennard Pill. Then over the stepping stones and back to Penmaen.

THE PENNARD CASTLE AND PARKMILL ROUTE

This alternative, which will take an extra hour or so, takes the well-worn path along the east side of Pennard Pill, under the spectre of the Pennard Castle almost up into Parkmill.

Before starting the uphill stretch to get into the village, it is sometimes possible to ford Pennard Pill at around MR 543890 to gain the old green lane which goes back to Penmaen through North Hills Farm.

If the river is too high you will need to go into Parkmill, then come out on to the main road towards Penmaen. The green lane starts from the main A4118 road just to the west of Parkmill. It goes steadily uphill leaving a dry valley on the right.

WINDING TO THE SEA - PENNARD PILL

It is full of garlic-smelling ramsons in the summer.

After bearing first to the left, then to the right, it passes deep between hedges on a typical green lane, reaching the plateau and gradually bearing further around to the right past a caravan site to reach North Hills Farm.

On the way you can hear the roar of the breakers in the bay and get a very fine view of Three Cliffs Bay.

From North Hills Farm it is an easy, slightly uphill walk back to Penmaen Church.

WHAT TO LOOK FOR

Geology Vertical limestone rock strata — the Three Cliffs peaks; great for sand dunes, caves, synclines and anticlines in rock strata.

Birds and other fauna Waders, sea birds, small mammals, sheep, wild horses.

History and pre-history Pennard Castle and ancient church ruins, earthworks and ancient village at Penmaen Burrows

Conservation Sand dunes and National Trust land acquisition.

Visual aspect Notthill *(National Trust)*, Castle and church.

Botany Limestone crags — harebell, white campion, red campion, red clover, bloody cranesbill, greater knapweed, common ragwort, field scabious, rose-bay willowherb, kidney vetch. Yellow whitlow grass *(rare)* on crags below Pennard Castle; Woodland — bluebells, ramsons, forget-me-not; Sand dunes and marshes — sea lavender, ox-eye daisy, foxglove, Isle of Man cabbage *(rare)*.

Nautical interest Large bulk carriers in the Bristol Channel, view of Devon coast and *(occasionally)* Lundy Island, fishing and sailing boats, pleasure cruisers Waverley or Balmoral.

SWEEPING VIEW - LANGLAND BAY

DISTANCE	2.4 MILES/4KM
TIME	2 - 3 HOURS
GRADING	1 - 2

OUTLINE If you stick to the main made-up lower path this is one of the easiest walks on Gower. It is ideal for a late summer's evening when you can enjoy the sunset over Cefn Bryn. On return, if you take the short steep climb out of Caswell Bay this will bring you up onto the clifftop walk past the golf course. Your reward is a slightly more difficult walk with splendid coastal views.

TRANSPORT

BUS No bus direct to Langland Bay but Caswell Bay buses can drop you at a convenient spot to walk to Langland.

CAR Take B4593 out of Mumbles and follow signposts to Langland Bay.

PARKING Large car park *(fee in summer daytime)* at Langland Bay.

HIDING AWAY - THE LONG-TAILED FIELDMOUSE

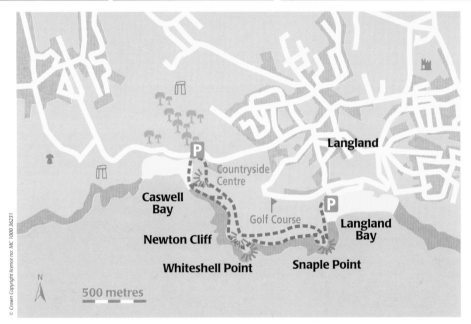

© Crown Copyright licence no: MC 1000 36231

Langland

P Countryside Centre

Caswell Bay

P **Langland Bay**

Golf Course

Newton Cliff

Whiteshell Point

Snaple Point

N

500 metres

WHERE TO START

The car park in Langland Bay.

LANGLAND BAY TO WHITESHELL POINT

From the car park go through one of the gaps in the beach huts to reach the tarmac beach path. Turn right and head towards the golf course.

The path soon curves around the western end of the bay and goes through a metal gate *(no cycles)*. It then goes very slightly uphill to reach your first spectacular viewpoint at Snaple Point. The view will depend on the weather and the tides and it is always different. It takes in the Bristol Channel and its shipping, the Devon coast and both ways along the Gower coast.

From the lookout, the generally easy and smooth path wends its way above the rocky shore.

Towards Whiteshell Point it deteriorates a little then takes a series of concrete steps up to a bend and another splendid view along the west coast *(if you wish to get to the upper path several tracks lead up the hill)*.

The view from this point over Caswell Bay and Pwlldu to Cefn Bryn can be quite breathtaking especially in the late evening with the sea shimmering in the glinting rays of the setting sun.

SEEING RED - A ROBIN

FLY AWAY HOME - A LADYBIRD

Enjoy the view for a few moments while you regain your breath. Then head south east along the top of the cliffs leaving a bungalow and a dilapidated stone wall on your left.

When you reach the western edge of the golf course head south towards Newton Cliff. Always keep clear of the fairway and the greens.

By all means have a chat with the golfers if they are of a mind to do so. But remember they have their minds on other things.

Do stop if it is clear that they are about to make a shot – although in many ways they are used to having walkers here and would just prefer you to carry on and get clear as soon as possible.

Newton Cliff is the one place where you may come into conflict with the golfers because it is not clear exactly where the path goes *(some judicious path clearing and signposting here would help both golfers and walkers)*.

The best thing is to wait for the golfers to get clear then go and enjoy the fine viewpoint. This is even better than the one on Whiteshell Point.

WHITESHELL POINT TO CASWELL BAY

The walk along the well-surfaced path to Caswell Bay gradually curves round into the bay then finally turns down an easy gradient past the café on your left to reach the main road.

The closer you get to Caswell Bay the easier it is to find access points over rocks to the beach or up through the gorse to the golf course. Care is needed in going down the rock scrambles to the beach and close attention needs to be paid to the state of the wind, tides and sea. There is a profusion of wild flowers along the path in spring and summer.

CASWELL BAY TO NEWTON CLIFF

You may return exactly the way you have just come. You will be more greatly rewarded, however, if you take the clifftop/golf course route. To reach this, walk about 100 metres up the road going back to Mumbles and Langland Bay.

Just before the Bishop's Wood Countryside Centre there is an unmarked path going up through thick woodland *(slippery when wet)*.

A short stiff zig-zag climb through bracken and sorrel brings you out onto a clearing, overlooking Caswell Bay.

path down through thick gorse and bracken to rejoin the main path near the metal gate.

To head home just take the good tarmac path round past the bathing huts and back to the car park.

It couldn't be easier and hopefully this will give you a stimulus for the more demanding Gower walks.

WHAT TO LOOK FOR

Geology, caves A bone cave was discovered at the eastern end of the bay *(known as Rotherslade or Little Langland),* named Rothers Tor Cave but was later filled in. Caswell Bay has an Iron Age earthwork *(situated on Redley Cliff).*

FAMILIAR SIGHT - A BLACKBIRD

NEWTON CLIFF TO LANGLAND BAY

From the vantage point you are almost home and dry. The walk is almost all level or downhill, leaving the golf course to your left. You still pass quite close to fairways and greens but they are easy to keep clear of from now on. The path takes you through bracken and grass over a series of hillocks until you reach the final one, overlooking Langland Bay.

After enjoying this final view you have two choices.

You may head straight down the slope to the path at Snaple Point.

Or, if it is not too wet, you can take the steeper and rougher

RARITY - AN ORCHID

Botany Orchids such as the early purple and pyramidal, viper's bugloss, heather, gorse, campion, harebells.

Birds and fauna Robins, blackbirds, stonechats, herring gulls, sparrows, magpies, seals off Snaple Point.

Visual aspect Views over Caswell Bay & Point and Pwlldu Head.

FLIGHT DISPLAY - A BUTTERFLY SPREADS ITS WINGS

DISTANCE	**2.7MILES/4.5KM**
TIME	**2 - 3 HOURS**
GRADING	**2**

OUTLINE This is a mainly woodland walk with generally easy gradients except for a steep climb at the finish. There are a few surprises, especially the view which suddenly comes up at Crawley Cliff. The upper path is slightly precarious in its early stages and the Crawley Woods path is somewhat overgrown. For the botanist there are a number of rare lime-loving plants — but you need to be an expert to find them.

TRANSPORT

BUS From Swansea Quadrant to Oxwich Bay or Port Eynon *(infrequent)*, alight at Nicholaston village.

CAR Take the A4118 out of Swansea to Parkmill. Continue through Penmaen for half a mile where you will come across a bus stop on the right and a turning to the right and another to the left. Take the right turn.

PARKING Immediately on your left after the right turn is a parking space for about 2 or 3 cars *(no charge)*.

SMALLEST BIRD - WREN

If you go down to the woods today

🚶 WHERE TO START

The bus stop at Nicholaston.

NICHOLASTON HAMLET TO CRAWLEY WOODS

Cross the main road carefully. Take the road going downhill *(no cars or motorcycles except for access)*, leaving a row of white cottages on your right. Bear to the right to reach a gate and a stone stile with signs for Nicholaston Burrows and Nicholaston Woods.

The left hand stepped path goes down to the burrows while the right hand farm track goes towards the woods. Keep along the farm track until you see a gate leading into a field and another farm track going off to the left. Take the latter then carry on past a small quarry and

sheep pen on your right and soon you will start on the true path. This winding, rocky and undulating path soon takes a sharp turn to the left.

WILDLIFE - A SQUIRREL HAS A SNACK

At this point, avoid the temptation to keep going downhill.

Dodge into the forest straight ahead along a delightful

wooded path until, in a few minutes, you burst out on to the top of Crawley Cliffs.

The path is indistinct in places and, if in doubt, keep to the right and go uphill.

This is one of the wilderness areas of Gower, with superb views over Nicholaston Pill and Oxwich Bay. There are many wild flowers in this area which you can, for a few brief moments, truly call your own.

The woods themselves are full of oak, ash and elm.

Do not be tempted to go down the cliffs. Turn back and head south in the woodland.

If you keep to the topmost path you will suddenly come out onto a second lookout on an outcrop of rocks. This one has views to both the east and west. Turn

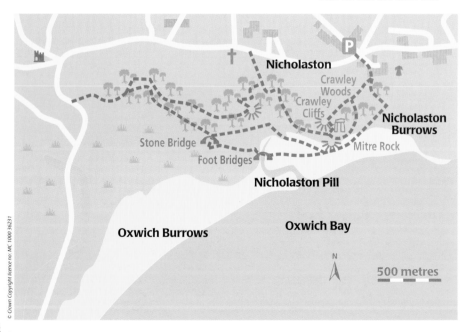

Nicholaston

Crawley Woods

Crawley Cliffs

Nicholaston Burrows

Stone Bridge

Foot Bridges

Mitre Rock

Nicholaston Pill

Oxwich Burrows

Oxwich Bay

N

500 metres

© Crown Copyright licence no: MC 1000 36231

FROND MEMORIES - THE HARTS TONGUE FERN

back from here and go steadily downhill until you come out just on top of the higher of the regular paths above Nicholaston Burrows. To be sure you are in the right place look for the small but distinctive Mitre Rock on the other side of the path.

CRAWLEY CLIFFS TO OXWICH BAY ROAD

Head in a general westerly direction on the well defined path, which has a steep cliff below to the left and rocky woodland to the right. Soon you are into woodland and then onto the prominent track, which comes down from the Church of St Nicholas.

Follow this track round, initially uphill then contouring round above the streams which lead down into Nicholaston Pill.

After several twists and turns and passing a prominent slab of rock, the path turns south-east and suddenly reaches a fine viewpoint looking back to Crawley Cliffs and Great and Little Tor.

From the lookout you have a gentle downhill walk through deciduous woodland.

At the end of this you will join the prominent main lower track.

You can join this or take a slight diversion, contouring to join the track 100 metres or so further on.

From here, it is a pleasant and easy walk on a good track to the gate and steps leading out on to the road going down to Oxwich Bay.

OXWICH BAY ROAD TO NICHOLASTON PILL

Start your return from the gate marked "Please do not block gate

– in constant use". There is also a green footpath sign and a National Nature Reserve Oxwich sign here. (It is possible to park outside the gate as long as you keep well clear of it. This is not an official car park and there is strictly no parking along the road down to Oxwich Bay). The track is clear and initially returns the way you have just come. It slowly drops down to marshland level.

Once the high road path has been lost to your left, the lowland path continues through dense woodland.

There are frequent views of the marshes and the Oxwich Burrows and soon your easy walking will bring you to a stone bridge on your right.

This goes over the main ditch draining the upper part of the marshes. The main Nicholaston Pill is a little further over towards the dunes.

LIFE IN DEATH - FUNGUS GROWS ON A ROTTING STUMP

NICHOLASTON PILL TO NICHOLASTON HAMLET

You have to choose here – the lower footpath route or the dune route. Both converge later on and both take you through the top of Nicholaston Burrows and back to the hamlet.

If you are taking the lower footpath route simply keep going on the path ahead. This takes you through more woodland then eventually out onto the edge of the burrows with the higher clifftop walk above you.

You will sight the Mitre Rock above then fight your way through the dunes to reach a point where you have to decide whether to bear left or right.

It does not really matter too much as long as you keep going upwards.

The right-hand fork is probably the better of the two since it will bring you onto the slatted path, which goes down to the sea.

It will also take you onto the steps by the stream, which runs down from the hamlet.

For the dune route, turn right over the bridge and then sharp left. Keep on going through reeds until the path bears around and then crosses over Nicholaston Pill by a small footbridge. Now bear around to the right on a more indistinct path, this time going from west to east.

You may choose here to go down to the wide expanse of beach or even double back across the burrows or beach to Oxwich. Our route takes us due east across a bigger footbridge over Nicholaston Pill then on quite a prominent track over the dunes with a variety of dune flowers and bushes. Soon you will join the lowland path route over the burrows.

If you should choose to bear to the left into woodland rather than heading across the dunes, this is no great loss. You will soon be faced with a stiff climb up through the woodland to the point where you departed earlier into Crawley Woods.

Once there retrace your steps back to Nicholaston hamlet and the bus stop.

WHAT TO LOOK FOR

Birds and other fauna
Grey squirrel, many species of butterfly, woodland fungi such as jew's ear and candle snuff fungi. Buzzard, owls, woodpeckers, nuthatch, wren, robins, tits, treecreeper.

FLORAL ARRANGEMENT - WOOD ANEMONE

History St Nicholas' Church *(Victorian gothic)* dates from 1894 although the original east window, chancel and some walling from the 14th Century can still be seen.

Conservation National Nature Reserve, Oxwich.

Visual aspect Views over Crawley Woods and Great and Little Tor.

Botany Wood anemone, yellow archangel, wood sorrel, hedge woundwort, a variety of dunes flowers, woods full of oak ash and elm. Mosses and ferns.

Geology Mitre Rock.

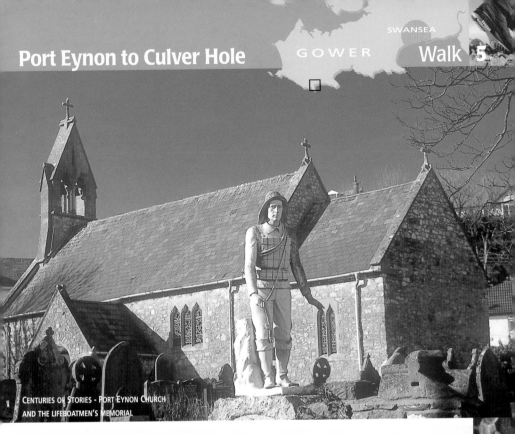

CENTURIES OF STORIES - PORT EYNON CHURCH
AND THE LIFEBOATMEN'S MEMORIAL

DISTANCE	**1.5MILES/2.5KM**
TIME	**2 HOURS (3 with diversions)**
GRADING	**2 OR 4 if taking the lower headland path**

OUTLINE A generally easy walk initially over beach and pebbles, then along the coast below the cliffs to Culver Hole. Return via Port Eynon Head and the quarries.

TRANSPORT

BUS No 18a from Swansea Quadrant *(infrequent)* to Port Eynon or the Gower Explorer No 18T on Sundays from June to September.

CAR By A4118 from Blackpill, Swansea, to the end of the road in Port Eynon.

PARKING Park by the sea front, where there are a few spaces, or in the large car park *(fee applicable in summer months)* next to the caravan park.

FLAVOUR OF THE PAST - THE SALT HOUSE

Salty taste of how life used to be lived

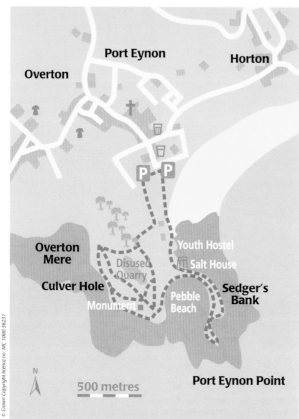

LANDSCAPE - TOWARDS PORT EYNON FROM PORT EYNON POINT,
WITH SEDGERS BANK IN THE FOREGROUND

© Crown Copyright licence no: MC 1000 36231

WHERE TO START

The beach car park – and head straight on to the beach.

PORT EYNON TO THE SALT HOUSE

There is an inland path if the tide is too high or the weather is too foul to go on the beach. Head due south to the youth hostel and keep going on the beach or path towards the Salt House, which is an old ruin by the seashore. Once past this you will reach a point where you are overlooking the pebble beach. You can turn right or left here. If you turn left, having carefully calculated the tide to make sure you do not get caught by rapidly rising waters, you can make your way out to Sedgers Bank. This diversion is well worthwhile, covering sand dunes and rocks exposed to varying degrees, depending on the state of tide.

Here there is a profusion of wild flowers adapted to the maritime environment.

This is a good place too to find all kinds of marine life and sea birds.

If you turn right, skirt round the well used path on the small cliff above the pebble beach. Soon you will have to decide whether to go straight up the ridge to get to The Monument – and then down to Culver Hole – or try the risky coastal route.

If in doubt take the easy option but if you do you will miss a delightful and slightly scary scramble over the lower headland.

Assuming you are taking the lower route, as you round the

CLIFF CONSTRUCTION - CULVER HOLE

headland look for the best footing for a rock scramble which takes you steadily upwards in a zig-zag over a series of limestone ledges. There is a cave and sometimes crashing waves beneath you, which you must ignore. Just keep going, keeping a good foothold all the time, and soon the worst is over and you are on a good safe coastal path. Do not be put off by this description because the little adventure is quite exhilarating and breathtaking. From here on, it is an easy jaunt to Culver Hole.

As you approach the deep fissure, which forms this distinctive landmark, the regular track down from the monument comes in from behind you on your right.

With the right state of tide you can go down a somewhat eroded track into the fissure and, if the fancy takes you, pick up a dangling rope and climb into the structure of Culver Hole.

CULVER HOLE TO THE MONUMENT

It is possible to return from Culver Hole to the Monument by a number of routes. You can, for example, go back via Overton or you can go various ways through the quarries.

We shall stick to the simple route. For this you turn back up the eroded path then head diagonally upwards to the left to a gap in the limestone crags.

Once you have reached this you can quickly head along the clifftop to The Monument. Curiously, this is made of granite, which is not a Gower stone.

The Monument itself was put up by the Gower Society in memory of Gwent Jones and Stephen Lee who *"helped to preserve these cliffs for the nation."*

This is a popular spot for all kinds of visitors, not all of them inveterate walkers.

In the course of an hour or so you can meet people here from all over the British Isles and often from abroad too.

THE MONUMENT TO PORT EYNON

The return to Port Eynon can be made by several different routes radiating out to the north, east and west from The Monument. The most frequently used one goes more or less north through gorse and bracken up and down over the disused quarry workings. This path soon heads downhill to a path, which runs alongside the camping fields — busy in summer but empty for the rest of the year.

Some 200 metres along this

HOMELAND - A WILD RABBIT

PRETTY POSY - GREAT MULLEIN

path there is a turning to the right, which heads straight down to the youth hostel.

Just before reaching the youth hostel you can turn to the left into the camp site and back to the car park –

or just go past the hostel onto the beach and return that way.

This walk may be crowded in the height of summer or on a Bank Holiday but that is no bad thing because you can meet some interesting people.

If you really want solitude there are many times, especially in bad weather, when there is nobody there at all.

You can take your pick and enjoy it, whichever you choose.

SETTING SEED - COMMON KNAPWEED

WHAT TO LOOK FOR

History and prehistory Eynon was a Welsh prince in the 11th Century and Port Eynon Castle (no longer present) is said to have been built by him. The Church of St Cattwg (renovated and enlarged in the 1860s) has an ancient stoup - a basin for holy water - in the porch, the gift of a shipwrecked Spanish captain. There is a buoy off Port Eynon Point marking the wreck of the Prince Ivanhoe.

Nautical interest Memorial statue at St Cattwg - remembering the members of the village lifeboat crew who drowned in 1916. In the 19th Century, limestone quarried on the spot was shipped across the Bristol Channel.

Geology Limestone quarries. Port Eynon Cave is a bone cave situated at the tip of the point - animal remains found. Culver Hole - one of the mysteries of Gower - is a 60ft wall built into the cliff. Its use is unknown but suggestions include a dovecote, a smugglers' retreat or it could have a earlier origin, linked to Port Eynon Castle or perhaps there was a linked passageway to the Salt House - who knows?

Birds Cormorants, oystercatchers, curlew, sanderling, rock pipit, turnstone.

Marine life Seals, variety of crustaceans, molluscs and annelids. Good for the rockpool explorer, excellent for sea weeds and lichen.

Botany Sea lavender, sea spurrey, sea thrift, common scurvy grass, great mullein, spring squill, sea campion, common rest harrow, large flowered evening primrose.

Visual aspect Views over Port Eynon Bay, Slade and Oxwich Point, also Overton.

Conservation The Monument was put up by the Gower Society in memory of Gwent Jones and Stephen Lee, founder members of the society.

ON THE BEACH - CASWELL BAY

DISTANCE	**2.7MILES/4.5KM**
TIME	**2 HOURS**
GRADING	**2**

OUTLINE This is an excellent and generally safe walk with splendid views of Caswell and Pwlldu Bay. On a good day there are impressive views of the Devon coast and shipping in the channel.

TRANSPORT

BUS Irregular services to Caswell Bay from Swansea's Quadrant bus station.

CAR Take B4593 from Mumbles to Caswell Bay.

PARKING Public car park in Caswell Bay MR 593877.
Fee payable 9am to 7pm, April 1 – September 30.

Parking is strictly forbidden virtually everywhere else in Caswell Bay.

FINERY - RED ADMIRAL BUTTERFLY

Just take a leap of faith and you'll be fine

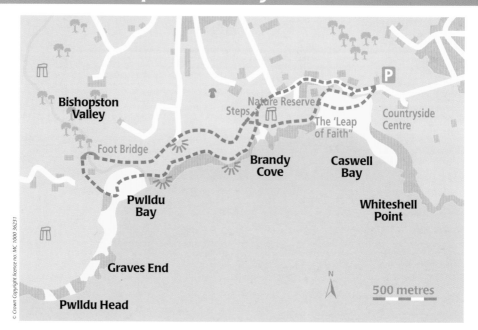

Bishopston Valley
Nature Reserve
Steps
The 'Leap of Faith'
Countryside Centre
Foot Bridge
Brandy Cove
Caswell Bay
Pwlldu Bay
Whiteshell Point
Graves End
N
Pwlldu Head
500 metres

© Crown Copyright licence no: MC 1000 36231

WHERE TO START

The phone boxes at Caswell Bay.

CASWELL BAY SECTION

Go uphill on the road to the west until you see a stepped path going down to the beach. At the bottom, proceed along the tarmac path at the top of the beach wall and below a large block of modern flats. At the end of this path there is a series of zig-zag steps which lead up to join the more prominent path coming in from the road on your right.

Turn left at the top into a wooded glade which overlooks Caswell Bay. Soon you will come to an exposed rocky outcrop with fine views over the sea. This is the *Leap of Faith*.

Take care going across this and you will then find yourself on a firm coastal path.

At half tide or lower you can walk straight across Caswell Bay

CLIFF-HANGERS - SCENERY AT SEVEN SLADES

beach to the zig-zag path which you can see in the north west corner of the bay.

THE LOWER COASTAL PATH

This is a well-defined path through gorse bush and ferns. Be careful of the cliff overhangs in places on your left although these are generally well protected by bushes.

Soon the path cuts inland to Brandy Cove and then out towards the sea. Here it is rougher and more rocky but still quite negotiable.

Once you are round the next headland, with fine views of Pwlldu Head and bay, the path again goes in and round a wide bay. At the next headland you can look right into Pwlldu Bay and clearly see your turning

SPRING SUPRISE - COWSLIPS

PWLLDU BAY

It is usually quite easy to cross the outlet of the Bishopston stream at the eastern end of Pwlldu Bay. Very occasionally, after heavy rains, the stream is running so fast you cannot cross it.

If this happens you must make your way back up to the track coming down from Pwlldu Lane.

point by the white cottages. Make your way on one of the several descent routes to get onto the shingle beach of Pwlldu.

Choose whichever way you fancy across the shingle. This is a two-steps-forward-one-step-back job but it does not take long to get to the other side. Now go along the dirt road between the cottages until you reach either the ford or the concrete footbridge over the Bishopston stream. Here you can rest for a while on a wooden bench and note the sign, which indicates that this is a National Trust area.

THE RETURN CLIFFTOP PATH

Several routes can be taken out of Pwlldu.

You can go up either side of Bishopston Valley or double back up a steep path to Pwlldu Head.

Our route up the four-wheel-drive road will take us in an easterly direction up to the clifftop walk.

When you have completed most of the climb, there is a stile on your right, which leads to an easy path out onto the prominent unnamed lookout at MR 580872.

This is an essential diversion as the views are brilliant.

Once you have enjoyed the views, turn inland and head along a well-defined and easy path in a generally easterly direction to the next headland.

This overlooks Brandy Cove to which you can descend if you wish down a straight grass slope.

It will give you the opportunity to return along the coastal path, which you came along earlier.

HEADS TOGETHER - COMMORANTS ON THE ALERT AT RING ROCK, PWLLDU

INSPIRING VIEW - A MAJESTIC SWEEP OF THE
GOWER COASTLINE, WITH PWLLDU BAY IN
THE FOREGROUND

INLAND ROUTE TO CASWELL BAY

If you cannot face the *Leap of Faith* at the end of the coastal pathway – and it is not really even a leap at all – then take the inland route.

The main attractions here are the wild flowers and a rather easy final section on the road.

From the headland go north east down a grassy slope into dense woodland into a series of gravel covered zig-zag steps. This brings you out over a stile into an open field then over another stile to reach the track going down from Bishopston to Brandy Cove.

Turn left through a gate then almost immediately right on this track then up a series of steps and a well-used path over a couple of stiles to reach the road which runs between Caswell Bay and Bishopston.

Once on the road it is an easy and steady walk back down to the car park – but beware speeding traffic. Face towards the oncoming vehicles.

There is a Glamorgan Wildlife Trust Conservation Area above Redley Cliff between Brandy Cove and Caswell Bay.

This is accessible from either bay but it should really be visited only in the company of experts.

WHAT TO LOOK FOR

Geology Pwlldu Bay is one of the best examples of a storm pebble beach. The parallel bands and ditches which run down the headland are the remains of extensive limestone quarrying in the 19th Century.

Visual aspect Views of coast looking back towards Swansea and the Devon coast on a clear day.

Botany Viper's bugloss, scabious, thrift, scarlet pimpernel, kidney vetch, gorse, heather, red campion, harebell, orchid, cranesbill, silverweed.

SHOWTIME - VIPER'S BUGLOSS

Birds and other fauna Choughs, stonechats,gulls, fulmars, cormorants.

History and pre-history Quarry on the eastern side of Pwlldu which not been worked since 1884. Ruined house on right hand side as you approach the beach.

Conservation Redley Cliff Conservation Area.

Nautical interest Pwlldu was once a thriving little port, with sailing brigs bringing in supplies and taking limestone to north Devon. There are many tales of smuggling.

Oxwich & Oxwich Castle

BREATHTAKING - THE VIEW TOWARDS OXWICH

DISTANCE	**3.4 MILES/5.5KM**
TIME	**2 - 3 HOURS**
GRADING	**3**

OUTLINE An exhilarating and energetic walk along well used and conserved paths and tracks. The early section is mainly undulating in woodland followed by a brief coastal jaunt and then a long, easy walk back past Oxwich Castle on a very good track.

TRANSPORT

BUS From Swansea's Quadrant to Oxwich *(infrequent)*.

CAR Take the A4118 from Swansea and turn left at the Oxwich Bay signpost, two miles beyond Nicholaston.

PARKING You have little choice here. You can either park in the Oxwich Bay Hotel *(free)* and take a drink or meal afterwards or park on the large, privately-owned beach park at MR 502865 (fee payable).

STRONGHOLD BY THE SEA - OXWICH CASTLE

Tread a fine line for your own safety

🚶 WHERE TO START

The car park at the Oxwich Bay Hotel.

OXWICH BAY TO OXWICH POINT

FROM the hotel go down the lane towards St Illtyd's Church. By the church gate, you will find a signpost reading "Horton 5.3km" and, a little later, a Countryside Council for Wales sign for Oxwich National Nature Reserve. Here the path bears to the right and goes directly up a series of 300 or so well graded steps. The path now bears to the left and picks up one of the many alternative paths. *(This one has come up through Oxwich woods from the road between Oxwich village and*

BREATHTAKING A VIEW FROM OXWICH POINT

Oxwich Green). Keep going on a slippery but well-worn path at the top of the woodland. After some 300 metres it bears to the left and skirts around the disused quarry below on your left *(there is an exciting and difficult path going straight back to St Illtyd's Church from here but it is not for the faint-hearted).*

With the quarry on your left, the path now descends a series of zig-zags, with steps and wooden railings in places. There is an ominous sign reading *"Dangerous edge – keep to main footpath",* which you ignore at your peril.

Keep going on the path which bears round to the right on reaching the coastal cliffs.

The path now undulates through woodland, going slightly uphill for a while until it comes out into scrubland.

It is difficult to define the exact position of Oxwich Point, which is probably just a little beyond the stile. From here there are good views back over Oxwich Bay and out into the Bristol Channel.

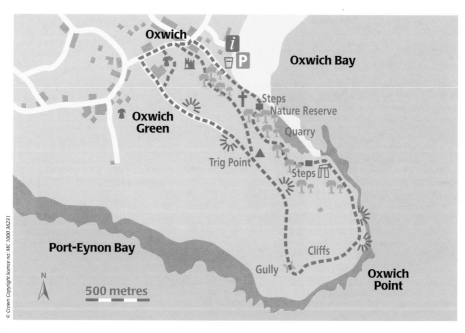

© Crown Copyright licence no: MC 1000 36231

GROWING WILD - THE COMMON SEA LAVENDER

OXWICH POINT TO OXWICH CASTLE

The path along the coast here is quite well worn, even if overgrown in places.

Conservation groups have made sterling efforts to keep the paths around Oxwich in good order. This path will shortly take you up through a gap in the cliffs and overland to Oxwich Castle. You could, of course, continue along the raised beaches of Port-Eynon Bay to Horton or you could do part of the walk then double back up one of the slades to Oxwich Green then back to Oxwich Bay. Not all of these slades are, however, official paths.

Many of these paths go through open farmland so do pay due respect to farm stock and crops as well as to the farmers.

Our return walk is much simpler, though it may be difficult to find the starting point to get through the gap in the cliffs. Around 300 metres or so beyond the stile look for an indistinct turning off the path to the right.

As you turn there are some bare limestone crags ahead of you. The path quickly turns left and then goes diagonally and steadily uphill (it does not matter if you miss this turning because there will soon be another opportunity to turn up towards the crags).

At the top of the incline, the path goes through a small gully with orange-stained rocks and out onto the gorse-ridden fields above. There are several waymarks which should help you on your way until you reach the farmtrack MR 507854.

At this point, note the fine views all around, but especially over Oxwich Bay.

Then bear to the left and continue on the path, leaving the Ordnance Survey triangulation point on your right. Continue along this track in a north westerly direction through gates and stiles until you reach Oxwich Castle.

FLOWER FORM - CLOSE-UP ON THE FLORA

OXWICH CASTLE TO OXWICH

The easiest way to get down to the village is to keep on down the road from the castle.

Then turn sharp right at the junction with the road between Oxwich Green and the village. Then simply carry on downhill to the village crossroads and then the car park.

There is an alternative, which seems to have fallen largely into disuse. This is a pity because it is a nice woodland walk.

It can be located by walking through the farmyard then taking a dip down towards the castle down an overgrown path until you locate the gully which takes you heading north-west down to the road. Look for the stile and you will find it.

WHAT TO LOOK FOR

Geology Limestone quarry. Limestone pavement formations at Oxwich Point.

Birds and fauna Herring gulls and black headed gulls, fulmar, cormorant, turnstone (*A diversion to the Oxwich Marsh and bird hides is a must for any keen bird watcher*).

Conservation National Nature Reserve.

WILD BUNCH - PRIMROSES

Botany Wood garlic, primrose, bluebells, snowdrops, wood anemone. Rarities like the bee orchid, water lily and marsh cinquefoil in Oxwich Marsh. Fungi such as cramp balls and cup shaped ascomycetes (*usually bright red*).

History A bay with a reputation for smugglers, once a port exporting limestone. John Wesley lodged and preached here at "The Nook" cottage. Church of St Illtyd, 12th Century. Many ships have been wrecked here — some, like the Solar, can still be seen. Oxwich Castle — 16th Century fortified Manor House.

SUNSET - THE END OF THE DAY

GOING WEST - ISLAND SUNSET

DISTANCE	3 MILES/5KM
TIME	2 - 3 HOURS
GRADING	2

OUTLINE A generally easy walk over dunes, beaches and clifftops. There are fine views towards Rhossili and Worm's

Head to the south and to west Wales and the Loughor Estuary to the north. There is the bonus of the magical island of Burry Holms with its rugged cliffs, sea birds, wild flowers and ancient heritage.

Note **Make sure you get the tides right before crossing over to Burry Holms. Allow three hours either side of low water for access** *(obtain tide times from the Evening Post or sports shops).*

TRANSPORT

BUS From Swansea Quadrant to Llangennith village. Then walk to Broughton Farm Caravan Park.

CAR Take the B4271 or B4295 to Llanrhidian then the minor roads to Llangennith and Broughton Farm.

PARKING Car park at MR 415924 – may be charged in the summer months.

AERIAL ACROBATICS - A FULMAR.

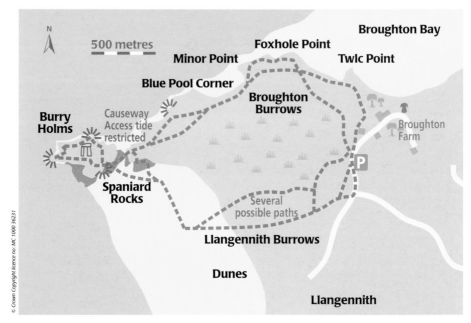

WHERE TO START

The car park at Broughton Farm.

ISLAND ADVENTURE - BURRY HOLMS

DUNES ROUTE FROM BROUGHTON FARM TO RHOSSILI BEACH

Head due west then south west along the edge of the dunes from the car park. After about 500 metres you will come across a stile from which there is a reasonably clear track heading west to the beach. If you go too far south you will get to the Llangennith (Hill End) car park. From here it is an easy walk to the beach. If you think you are lost on the dunes just keep going west to the sound of the surf (a compass can be useful). Have confidence and you will suddenly find yourself on the beach.

BEACH SECTION

This is an easy walk, heading north west towards Burry Holms which is only a few hundred metres away. As long as you have worked out the tides, you can take any route across the sand and rocks of the passage between Spaniard Rocks and Burry Holms.

COASTLINE - BROUGHTON BAY

BURRY HOLMS —
THE MAGIC ISLAND

Once on the island you can walk up the middle or around either side. An hour or two on the island is a delight. On the south side there are sheer cliffs with rocky promontories while the north side is a little easier. There is some good rock scrambling – with great care – on the north west spur. In spring and summer there is a superb display of wild flowers.

A profusion of gulls may be seen at any time. There are also several ancient buildings to be explored.

BURRY HOLMS TO
BROUGHTON FARM

From the crossing point at Spaniard Rocks go straight up the cliff path to the north-east, keeping the coast on your left hand side.

The path is quite distinct most of the way and eventually ends in a wooden slatted path leading down to the Broughton Farm Caravan Park *(fixed site)*.

It is easy to divert onto the dunes on your right.

If you do so, you may eventually end up in the car park. If in any doubt just turn back in a northerly direction towards the coast.

If you take any of the lesser paths to the left, they will usually bring you out on to the cliffs overlooking the sea.

Two diversions are worth taking.

One is to Culver Hole and Three Chimneys, the other is to the Blue Pool.

The diversion to Culver Hole MR 406930 is down a short steep track *(not recommended)* and can be approached at low water from both Llangennith sands and Broughton sands. The natural arch and the rock formation are well worth the effort and if the tide is low you can walk back to Broughton Farm along the beach.

The diversion to Blue Pool MR 409931 is down another short but steep track, which brings you to the unique and quite dramatic natural rock pool.

BEACH BOUQUET - SEASIDE PANSY

WHAT REMAINS? - THE BASE OF THE OLD BURRY HOLMS LIGHTHOUSE

WHAT TO LOOK FOR

Geology Burry Holms is a small limestone island. It has an Iron Age earthwork, viewed as a single bank and ditch which bisects the island. It also has the ruins of a medieval monastic settlement which may be connected with a pilgrimage associated with the Sixth Century St Cenydd. In sand dunes near Blue Pool Bay there are the remains of a stone-walled Iron Age enclosure. Culver Hole is a bone cave where the remains of more than 30 individuals were found. Blue Pool is a rock pool which measures around 15ft across where numbers of gold doubloons *(coins)* were once found. Three Chimneys is a fine natural archway.

Nautical interest Several small wooden shipwreck remains. Broughton Bay saw 16 vessels outward-bound from Llanelli wrecked on the same tide in 1868.

Botany Rock samphire grows on cliffs and flowers from July to October, also sea lavender, sea spurrey, sea thrift, burnet rose, vetch, orchids and harebells. Rockpools galore.

Fauna Rabbits, grass snakes, seals, passing porpoise.

Visual aspect Tremendous views over to Caldy Island and Tenby, also back over Rhossili Bay to Worm's Head.

Birds and other fauna Herring gulls, cormorants, shags, curlew, fulmar, snipe and pheasant.

Did you know? Holm is the ancient Norse appellation meaning island — however, there is no archaeological evidence to show that the vikings ever landed at Burry Holms. An automatic lighthouse once present there has been removed.

This is well exposed at mid to low tide and has a deep blue colour in certain conditions of sea and sky cover. It is popular for swimming and diving although care is needed in these activities.

From the path at the top of the Blue Pool there are signposts which confirm you are on the right track.

Soon you will be on the path with the wooden slats. From here, it is an easy downhill walk back to the car park.

FLUTTER BY - FIVE-SPOTTED BURNET MOTH

SUNDAY LLANRHIDIAN CHURCH

DISTANCE	3.5MILES/5.6KM
TIME	2 HOURS
GRADING	2

OUTLINE A splendid quiet easy walk for a warm summer's evening. It takes in a lovely church, ancient castle, woodland glades, coastal tracks and numerous field crossings, stiles and farmsteads.

TRANSPORT

BUS Number 17 from Swansea's Quadrant *(infrequent)* and get out at Llanrhidian or take the Gower Explorer on Sundays and bank holidays in summer *(two per day)*.

CAR Take B4295 from Gowerton or B4271 from Killay on outskirts of Swansea. At the junction, where these turn into minor roads, turn right immediately into Llanrhidian village.

PARKING Park by the village green outside the church at MR 498923.

WATER FEATURES - FROST SPARKLES ON A CUCKOO FLOWER

WORK PLACE - A MILL POND IN LLANRHIDIAN

WHERE TO START

The village green in the heart of Llanrhidian.

LLANRHIDIAN TO WEOBLEY CASTLE

Go into the churchyard through the heavy black gates. Go past the church to the left-hand corner and over a stone stile onto the path ahead. Go over a small stream with a stone-walled millpond to the right. Leave a disused quarry on your left to reach a paved road coming in from the right. Here you will pick up a signpost saying Weobley Castle 2km. The road deteriorates to a gravel track leaving tracks going down to Staffal Haegr. It soon becomes a single track leading over a stile into a rough field. After the next stile continue across another field and over two stiles near a clump of trees and into a grassy lane.

Once over another stile, with a signpost saying "Leason Wood 250m," you will get the first of many spectacular views of the stark and foreboding Weobley Castle.

An easy walk under the hill with dense woodland to your left brings you to another stile and enters a narrow pathway which is fenced and wooded on both sides. It is full of wild flowers in the spring.

On reaching the end of this path there is a small pond on your right MR 483927. Go over another stile, then up a rough track leading uphill to the southwest. Within a few metres there is a stile leading off to the right into woodland, quickly followed by another stile leading into a long, wide field with views of the castle above you.

Near the end of this field, you can divert away to the left to take the path below the castle to reach the rough farm track leading down to Llanrhidian Marsh.

Turn left up the farm track MR 477929 and go steadily uphill to reach the entrance to Weobley Castle (This is one of the few climbs that you have on this walk).

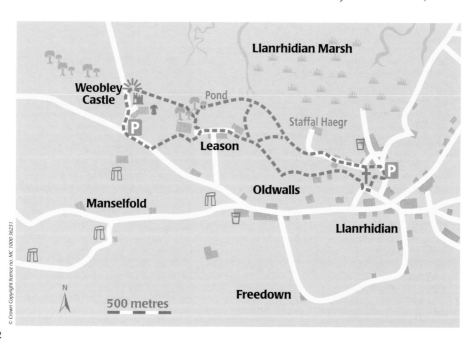
Llanrhidian Marsh
Weobley Castle
Pond
Staffal Haegr
Leason
Oldwalls
Manselfold
Llanrhidian
Freedown
500 metres
N

DOWN TO THE SEA - ESTUARY LANDSCAPE NEAR WEOBLEY

WEOBLEY CASTLE TO LEASON

After a break at the castle, which is open from 9.30am to 6.30pm *(fee to be paid)*, go to the stout wooden seat on the seaward outside of the castle walls. Enjoy the stupendous view across the Loughor Estuary to Burry Port and Llanelli, or up the estuary towards the Black Mountains or out to the west to the Whiteford lighthouse and across the Towy estuary to the Preseli Mountains, 50 km away.

Now you are ready for the easy, but slightly confusing in places, walk back across country to Llanrhidian. Make your way to the main road, turn left then after about 300 metres go to the left at one of the newer green footpath signs MR 479924.

Go over a series of stiles in a generally northeasterly direction to reach the outer walls of the Leason Farm complex. Go over a double stile onto a muddy track, which changes to gravel then tarmac.

Keep on the tarmac heading generally eastwards through the Leason hamlet *(with barking dogs at every move)* until you reach an old cottage at the eastern end of the track. Here you can, if you wish, return down an ancient pathway to reach the coastal path at 250 metres, signposted at MR 486925.

HILLTOP FORTRESS - WEOBLEY CASTLE

STILL STANDING - THE OLD WHIPPING STONES AT LLANRHIDIAN CHURCH

WHAT TO LOOK FOR

Birds Heron, thrush, blackbird, nuthatch, owl, buzzard. Wintering wildfowl out on the marsh.

Fauna Fungi plentiful — cramp balls, small woodland rodents.

Visual aspects Views of Weobley Castle on the approach and fine views over the estuary.

Botany Cuckoo flower, yellow pimpernel, self heal, ground ivy, red campion, navelwort, yellow iris, cow parsley, many varieties of trees, ferns and mosses.

LINING THE LANES - HERB ROBERT

History and pre-history
Weobley Castle, a 13th-14th Century fortified manor house, 13th Century Llanrhidian Church — carving in the porch known as the Leper Stone, believed to date from the 9th Century. Mill race and pond, old farm buildings and ancient pathways. Llanrhidian — a north Gower estuarine village, once a centre for family weaving and sheep rearing. Several ruins of corn and woollen mills. Standing stone on the green may be the remains of a village cross known as the Whipping Stone, used as a pillory before the 19th Century. There were two mills on the stream which runs through Llanrhidian — now only the Nether Mill remains.

LEASON TO LLANRHIDIAN

To take the main inland path back to Llanrhidian take the stile to your right into a large field. Then turn left and head across the field keeping the fences fairly close to your left.

Keep in the fields, going over two more stiles, until you reach a hedge where you have to turn right or left. By going right you can quickly get to Oldwalls and the Greyhound Pub.

Do not be distracted for our walk is almost over and the last bit is quite an adventure. Turn left over another stile, head down the side of the field over another stile, which takes you into a wooded area with a clearing. Bear to the right and over a mini-ford by a small pool. Then continue uphill until you go through a gap into a field with grazing horses. Go over a stile into a rough rocky field where the path skirts around the north side of Penrhallt Farm.

Some of this path has been restored with waymark signs so you should not lose your way too easily. Now head through an overgrown field over another stile and into a recently renovated farm yard which formerly kept much ancient farm machinery.

Cross Pen-yr-Allt Farm yard, leaving the cottage on the left and entering a distinct track with a carefully rebuilt dry stone wall. This takes you past a gate onto a path, which quickly brings you on to some limestone crags overlooking Llanrhidian.

The path skirts round a quarry on your left and then enters the top end of the village. As soon as you hit the road turn left then follow the road down past the chapel and Post Office to reach your starting point at the village green.

SUNSET STRONGHOLD - OYSTERMOUTH CASTLE

DISTANCE	3MILES/5KM
TIME	2 - 3 HOURS
GRADING	1 AND 2

OUTLINE An easy if crowded walk along the seafront to begin with. Then there is a short steep climb up to the top of the inner Mumbles Head. This is followed by a slightly longer climb to get up to the top of Mumbles Hill – everywhere with a splendid all round view over Swansea Bay, the Bristol Channel and down the Gower Coast. The last part of the walk entails a meander around the houses and a couple of woodland stretches before taking on the delights of Oystermouth Castle followed by another brief woodland interlude before returning to the bayside path.

TRANSPORT

BUS From Swansea Quadrant (nos 1,2,3,37) frequent service. Alight at Oystermouth Square.

CAR A4067 along Swansea Bay from the city centre.

PARKING Can be a lottery. There are many spaces and you just have to try your luck. Some are fee paying others are free. Much less of a problem out of season.

STRETCH OF SAND - SWANSEA BAY

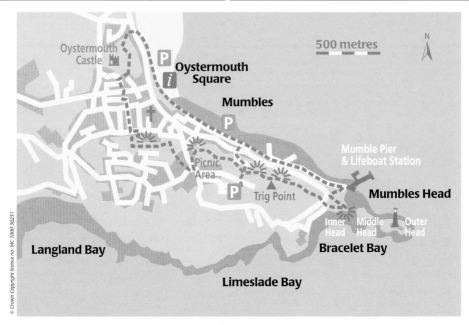

Oystermouth Castle

P

Oystermouth Square

ℹ

Mumbles

P

500 metres

N

Mumble Pier & Lifeboat Station

Picnic Area

P

Trig Point

Mumbles Head

Inner Head Middle Head Outer Head

Langland Bay

Bracelet Bay

Limeslade Bay

© Crown Copyright licence no: MC 1000 36231

WHERE TO START

From Oystermouth Square, Mumbles.

OYSTERMOUTH SQUARE TO MUMBLES HEAD

This is the easiest bit – except for the end. Head south east towards Mumbles Head on the bayside path. In the early stages this is a combined cycleway/walkway. It can be congested and you will have to be patient with occasional inconsiderate cyclists and in-line skaters *(the majority take great care to avoid the walkers).*

There are many things to see en route but your first main landmark will be the boat launching slipway at Verdi's ice cream parlour. After that you may lose some of the cyclists but you'll have to mix with the yachties and fishermen and, later, the jet-skiers.

Once past these you join the cars and strollers going to the cafe and amusement arcade at Mumbles Pier *(well worth the diversion since a splendid overhaul and despite the fact that pleasure steamers visit only rarely).*

Now for the short sharp shock. Go up some stone steps opposite the cafe and keep going until you reach the small car park above. Now turn back and take in the splendid view of Swansea Bay.

Then head up one of the short tracks up to the top of the inner Mumbles Head.

MISTY OUTLINE - MUMBLES HEAD

GATEWAY - THE IMPOSING FRONT ENTRANCE TO OYSTERMOUTH CASTLE

The right hand path takes you diagonally down the hill through woodland to reach The George pub and the bayside path. The middle path has been carefully graded for the use of prams and wheelchairs.

Enjoy this luxury while it lasts. When the graded path turns off to the left our path goes round to the right past an old kiln and then to the left above a wooded gully.

This path is still in good condition and well used. There is a profusion of wild flowers in this area in spring and summer. Leave the mobile homes/caravan park to your left and soon the path will come out into an open grassy space.

Here you will get an even better view than before, taking in all of Swansea Bay, the Bristol Channel and the south Gower coast.

There is invariably some shipping activity off Mumbles Head in the channel.

Note At low tide *(two hours either side of low water)* you can go across the rocks and shingle to the middle and outer heads. There are certain restrictions around the lighthouse but you can wander almost anywhere around and on top of the two heads. Do not get caught in any of the tide rips – they are powerful here.

MUMBLES HEAD TO MUMBLES HILL

From the Mumbles Head car park cross the road by the Big Apple ice cream kiosk *(a one-time navigation buoy).* Go straight up the rocky zig-zag path, keeping on the Swansea Bay side all the time going up the ridge. The little climb will be easy for the regular coastal walker but it may cause some trouble to the less fit.

This is the biggest climb on the whole walk – although there are still a few more climbs to come.

Enjoy the superb views until you reach the official top of the hill – the Ordnance Survey triangulation point at MR624876.

WALK ON WATER - MUMBLES PIER

MUMBLES HILL TO OYSTERMOUTH CASTLE

If you want to sit down for refreshment carry on a little further to a pair of seats with another fine view. Here the path divides into three.

The one to the left goes to a small car park which is useful to anyone who wants to avoid the climb.

Follow some cottages on your left into Thistleboon Road.

Before entering the road you may care to take a brief deviation to your right.

Here you will come into a delightfully conserved picnic area with a barbecue stand and a most photogenic view looking down on to Mumbles village *(Oystermouth)* and the castle.

NIGHTFALL - MUMBLES AT DUSK

This is actually public land but it is lovingly looked after by neighbouring householders.

Once into Thistleboon Road go up the hill and turn sharp right then sharp right again into Western Close. Go to the end of the close and take the footpath to the left of the end house.

Continue along this path, with houses on both sides, until it starts to go steadily uphill, bearing to the left.

You now have woodland *(good for bluebells)* on your right and a garden on your left. Soon you will have another superb view straight across the village to Oystermouth Castle and Swansea Bay.

To get to the castle carry on along your path for about 200 metres. Then turn right down a steep slippery woodland path with metal railings.

Once you are onto Overland Road turn left. Within 100 metres or so turn sharp right into Woodville Road.
Now follow your nose to the Castle from which you will again get more brilliant views all over Mumbles.

OYSTERMOUTH CASTLE TO OYSTERMOUTH SQUARE

If you are exhausted you can just turn back down Castle Avenue into Newton Road and back to Oystermouth Square.

However, there is a good alternative. Go to the top north east corner of the Castle grounds.

Make your way down one of several possible routes through woodland, then a grassy path, then more woodland to reach the main coast road.

Cross this with great care and you are back on the bayside walkway and cycleway.
It is now a short hop back to Oystermouth Square.

WHAT TO LOOK FOR

Geology Prominent limestone islets. On the outer islet is Mumbles Lighthouse, built in 1793, and a coast defence fort *(1861)*.

Birds and other fauna Many species of gull, waders at low tide such as plover, curlew, godwits, redshank common clifftop birds such as stonechat, pipits, blackbird, dunlin, sparrow.

Botany Foxgloves, bloody cranesbill, pimpernel, herb robert, harebells, orchid, clover, knapweed.

Conservation Nature Reserve; Mumbles Hill. Oystermouth Square redevelopment — a lost opportunity for a tasteful and considerate reuse of an important Swansea Bay heritage site.

Visual aspect Numerous viewpoints. From the inner Mumbles Head you have a splendid view of all of Swansea Bay.

Nautical interest Mumbles Pier; Mumbles Lifeboat Station; Shipping in the bay; Mumbles Lighthouse.

History Oystermouth Castle was built around 1100 but destroyed by fire in 1116. It was rebuilt but destroyed again by fire 1216. It was rebuilt and destroyed again. The present stone keep was damaged but repaired and a few years later a gatehouse and curtain wall were built. A chapel block was added and the keep remodelled — the castle served as a prison and courthouse for many years.

LOOKING BACK - VIEW FROM THE WORM.

DISTANCE	**4.5 MILES/7.2KM**
TIME	**2 HOURS**
GRADING	**2 - 3**

OUTLINE This walk is one of the first that should be completed by any aspiring Gower coastal walker. It is seldom very crowded but people who do use it are very friendly, passing on advice about the tides, the blowhole and how to cross the Devil's Bridge. It is quite a tough walk in parts. It is a variety of coastal path, rock scrambling, moorland walking, ridge walking and exhilarating seascapes. Children will find this an enjoyable and challenging walk but any under about 12 will struggle on parts.

TRANSPORT

BUS Take the bus *(infrequent)* from Swansea Quadrant to Rhossili terminus.

CAR Take A4118 from Swansea, then turn right on B4247 at Scurlage to end of road at Rhossili.

PARKING Private carpark opposite hotel, fee payable.

Note **It is requested that walkers do not tackle the Outer Head during the bird breeding season from March 15 to July 15 unless with a group of recognised birdwatchers.** The causeway is only open for two hours either side of low water. Make a start during the earlier part of the opening. **On return allow at least half an hour before the published causeway closing**

time. Find this out from the NT visitor centre or on a board at the Old Coastguard Lookout or by working it out from the tide tables.

DRY DOCK - AN ANCHOR AT WORM'S HEAD, BELIEVED TO BE FROM THE SAMUEL.

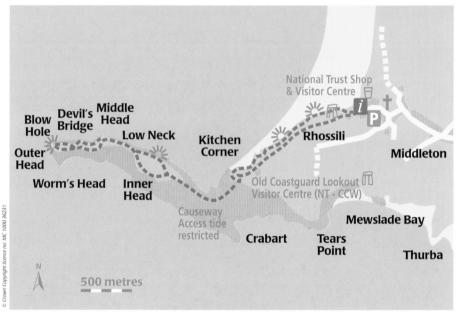

National Trust Shop
& Visitor Centre

Blow Hole Devil's Bridge Middle Head Low Neck Kitchen Corner Rhossili

Outer Head Middleton

Worm's Head Inner Head Old Coastguard Lookout Visitor Centre (NT - CCW)

Causeway Access tide restricted Crabart Tears Point Mewslade Bay Thurba

N

500 metres

© Crown Copyright licence no: MC 1000 36231

WHERE TO START

The National Trust Shop and Visitor Centre.

THE CAUSEWAY

Head for the National Trust shop. Walk along the regular path towards Worm's Head.
At the end take the zig-zag path straight down to the shoreline and make your way down to the causeway. You have a number of possible routes across this isthmus and stout boots are a decided advantage. Once across the causeway bear right then make for the first of the several islands which make up Worm's Head. The best way to tackle these rocks is to choose a line and stick to is as long as possible. It is a toss up whether you scramble over the larger rocks or keep going on the smaller boulders, dipping from time to time through rock pools.

THE INNER HEAD

Once onto the dry land take the right hand path *(the other one goes round the coastal route)* and climb up a series of limestone ledges to the top of the ridge.

Keep walking over and down the ridge to the first of a series of jagged rocky outcrops which join the Inner and Middle Heads. Soon a more prominent rock path will be reached.

Follow this and then turn sharp left over the distinctive Devil's Bridge onto the larger part of Middle Head. You may now go with care straight up and right along the ridge. Or you can go round the level coastal path to the rocky crossing

between the Middle and Outer Heads. With the right tide and weather you will see a distinctive blow hole. Before you descend that far there is also a mini-cave which opens out to a view out towards Burry Holms. There is a steep drop below there so do not go too far.

SUNBATHER - A SEAL

LORD OF ALL - A SEAGULL SURVEYS THE SCENE

THE OUTER HEAD

The Outer Head is worth attacking even if you feel exhausted. It is well worth the last zig-zag rock climb of 20 metres to the top for here you will see spectacular rocks, a good array of sea birds and magnificent views out to sea — especially good at sunset.

Even better is to go that last little bit down on to the first sloping ledge right at the end of the head. From here you will be rewarded with a spectacular downward view of crashing seas, jagged, lichen-covered rocks and sea birds.

Take great care especially on the northern side as the rock face here falls nearly vertically into the sea.

ROCK HARD - WORM'S HEAD AT LOW TIDE

ENCHANTING OUTLOOK - RHOSSILI BAY

THE RETURN

The return may be taken using the lower of the paths each time there is a choice.

It is also possible to bypass a couple of the islands by going over the rocks – but this is generally slower and more exhausting than the upper tracks.

The return to the inner head can be eased by taking the outer, generally level and easy, walking track back to the end of the island to tackle the 20 minutes or so of the balancing act back across the causeway.

The easiest return to the coastguard hut is the zig-zag – but the coastal path along the raised beach offers opportunities for a different return to Rhossili, Middleton or Pitton.

Note that when you are walking from Rhossili to the causeway you are on the final part of the *Gower Way* which was inaugurated by the Gower Society along with many other organisations and opened by the Prince of Wales on Cefn Bryn in 1998.

The Millennium Project starts at Penlle'r Castell in Upper Gower, passes through Felindre, Gowerton, Three Crosses and Parc le Breos, goes over Cefn Bryn and ends in Rhossili opposite Worm's Head.

WHAT TO LOOK FOR

Geology A mile-long promontory at the most westerly tip of the peninsula *(Viking word "wurm" meaning dragon)* which gets cut off at high tide. Between middle and outer heads is Devil's Bridge *(a bridge of rock)* and on the outer head is a booming blow hole. There is a cave on the outer head which faces out to sea. It is difficult to access and can only be viewed from the sea. Bones have been found here, including those of the rhinoceros and mammoth as well as human bones and flints. Worm's Head is a nature reserve rich in plant and bird life.

SEA EGGS - A CLUSTER OF EGGS OF THE COMMON DOG WHELK.

Birds and other fauna Seals, fulmar, common scoter, gulls, rock pipits, auks, oystercatcher, curlew, redshank, turnstone. Great rockpools for hermit crabs, limpets, sea anemone, seaweed.

Conservation National Trust nature reserve.

Visual aspect Fantastic views of Rhossili, Rhossili Bay, Burry Holms, Lundy and Caldy islands.

Botany Sea thrift, sea lavender, common scurvy grass, spring squill, clover, bloody cranesbill, kidney vetch, bird's foot trefoil, campion.

STORM TOSSED - LLANGENNITH AND THE CITY OF BRISTOL WRECK

A GOOD DAY - A SURFER WATCHES THE SUNSET AT RHOSSILI

DISTANCE	4 MILES/6.4KM
TIME	2 - 3 HOURS
GRADING	2

OUTLINE An exhilarating summer evening's walk.
It is generally easy walking with clear tracks, rough in a few places. There is a short, stiff climb at the beginning but after that only minor ups and downs. There are some quite breathtaking views over Rhossili and Worm's Head. There are equally impressive views back across the whole of Gower and way over to the north and west to the Black Mountains, Preseli Mountains and Pembrokeshire on a good day. There is the bonus of watching hang gliding and visiting the Helvetia wreck. Rhossili Down is to be avoided in foul weather or in sea mists unless you want to practise compass navigation.

TRANSPORT

BUS From Swansea Quadrant to Rhossili *(infrequent)*.

CAR A4118 out from Swansea, turn onto B4247 at Scurlage.

PARKING The official car park *(fee-paying in summer)*. Parking is difficult or forbidden anywhere else in Rhossili.

BLOWING THEIR OWN TRUMPETS - SEA BINDWEED

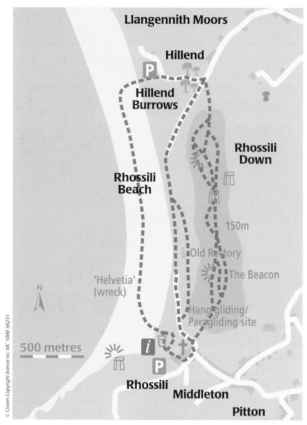

Llangennith Moors

Hillend

Hillend
Burrows

Rhossili
Beach

Rhossili
Down

150m

'Helvetia'
(wreck)

Old Rectory

The Beacon

Hang gliding/
Paragliding site

N

500 metres

© Crown Copyright licence no: MC 1000 36231

Rhossili
Middleton

Pitton

shall return on later. Now for the stiff climb. Follow the other signpost (also "Hill End") up some wooden steps then steadily uphill on a wide track. There are several different routes here but it is best to keep on the seaward side where you will see more of the hang gliders.

It is not too long before you reach the Ordnance Survey triangulation point at The Beacon. This is the highest point on Gower at 193 metres. From here you have a good all-round view of all Gower as well as down on to Rhossili and Worm's Head.

If that is not enough, on a good day, you can also see over the Loughor Estuary and Carmarthen Bay to the hills of Pembrokeshire and the Black Mountains.

From The Beacon head to the north on a good track past many of the distinctive rocks and stone of the old red sandstone conglomerates.

The track passes several well-weathered cairns on your right then splits into two. The right hand fork is the easy route, which takes you straight across the down. The left-hand fork takes you up a slight incline to another fine viewpoint.

From here, you can see Llangennith ahead and to your right and the islet of Burry Holms ahead and to your left. Go steadily downhill to rejoin the main path. Soon you will cross a couple of indistinct paths going down to the beach.

WHERE TO START

The official car park in Rhossili village.

RHOSSILI TO HILL END

From the car park walk up the main road past the church on your left. Then bear to the left to reach a lane leading due north (and going slightly downhill) to Rhossili Down. *There is a short cut around the north side of the church.* Keep on down the lane, past a track to the left with signposts for Rhossili Beach. Carry on to a

LAND'S END - WORM'S HEAD FROM RHOSSILI DOWNS

kissing gate/wooden gate beyond which the track splits into two — both are bridleways. The left-hand path signposted "Hill End" takes you below the down to the Old Rectory and beyond — this is the path we

ACROSS THE ESTUARY - THE VIEW FROM RHOSSILI DOWNS TOWARDS LLANGENNITH BURROWS AND BURRY HOLMS.

Then you reach a much more prominent track coming across the down from the south-east. This goes diagonally down to the left to a somewhat unsightly ruin of an old Second World War radar station.

From this prominent crossroads you can again take the easy route bearing to the right over the downs then take the steep descent into Hill End.

The much more interesting walk is to take the left-hand fork over the jagged fortress of rocks ahead. This is the only bit of rock scrambling you will get on this walk but it is well worth the diversion. There is no official name to this edge, which should be called Stony Edge because of its rock formation.

You now have another choice. Head straight on to rejoin the main path or – much better – deviate yet again to the left. Go gently uphill until you reach a small brick ruin – another

wartime relic – among square-shaped blocks of conglomerate rocks. This too is worth the diversion because of its fine views. Now it is downhill. Continue steadily down along the rocky edge until you rejoin the main path coming in from the right. Descend down a wide gully towards the entrance of the Hill End Caravan Site. Note the distinctive castellated edge to your right which looks just like the man-made buttress of a hill fortress. Soon your downhill canter is over and you are on a short grassland walk to the five-bar gate with a walkers' gate to the left and a National Trust sign saying: "Rhossili Down."

HILL END TO RHOSSILI

Take the path in a southerly direction, leaving the caravan and camp site on your right. This is an easy walk on a good path. It is level at first then slowly climbs past the Old Rectory to rejoin your outward

route at the rocket station.

During the walk you will cross a number of streams. There are also at least two places where you can cross over a stile into neighbouring fields and down to a parallel running lower path. This path, in turn, has tracks down to the beach. There are lots of cliff overhangs in one or two places so care is needed here.

PRICKLY CUSTOMER - SEA HOLLY.

GIANT'S GRAVE - THE WRECK OF THE HELVETIA ON RHOSSILI BEACH

WHAT TO LOOK FOR

Geology Impressive rock formations of Old Red Sandstone conglomerates.

Birds and animals Buzzards, kestrels, pipits, wheatears, skylark. Rabbits plentiful, foxes, wild ponies, sheep, small rodents such as shrews and mice. Lizards and snakes.

Conservation National Trust.

Visual aspect Fine views of Lundy island on a clear day.

Botany Sea bindweed, sea holly, sea stock, gorse, heathers, stonecrop.

History and pre-history Rhossili Church with a memorial to Petty Officer Edgar Evans, member of Scott's ill-fated expedition to the South Pole. Numerous cairns and ancient settlements, in particular the Sweyns Houses (*Sweyn being a Scandinavian sea lord who may have given his name to Swansea*).

Nautical interest The rocket station where lines could be fired to ships in distress and a breeches buoy rigged to rescue the crew, the Old Rectory was long occupied by the rector of the parish and also thought to have been a haven for smugglers. It remained empty for years but has now been restored by the National Trust. Shipwrecks include: Helvetia — wrecked in 1887 and still visible; City of Bristol — wrecked in 1840 and visible at low tide; The Dollar Ship — large quantities of coins found in 1807 and 1833.

BEACH WALK

From Hill End go down the road towards the sea, leaving the caravan site on your left. Go past the surfers' car park and over the dunes on a slatted path to the beach. Once there and clear of the surfies you will probably have the beach to yourself until you get to Rhossili. Enjoy the walk and the splendid, ever-changing view of Worm's Head and Rhossili cliffs.

If the tide is right, and it is only in exceptionally high tides and rough seas that you cannot walk the beach, divert to the wreck of the Helvetia.

Once you get onto the Rhossili end the path back to the village is distinct and well used.

CARPET OF FLOWERS - HEATHER AND GORSE

STEADY AS A ROCK - LLANMADOC CHURCH

DISTANCE	**6.5MILES/10.5KM**
TIME	**3 - 4 HOURS**
GRADING	**2**

Note **If you want to go round the lighthouse start your walk two to three hours before low water. This will allow you to arrive around an hour before low water and give plenty of time to get safely round the lighthouse**

Outline This walk is mostly flat on good tracks over sea walls through woodland and sand dunes going out. There is then a tidal section over sand and rocks followed by a long return on the sandy beach. If you have any energy left a small diversion up, Cwm Ivy Tor will bring the reward of fine views and a profusion of wild flowers.

TRANSPORT

BUS From Swansea's Quadrant to Llanmadoc *(infrequent).*

CAR B4295 from Gowerton or B4271 from Killay on outskirts of Swansea to Llanrhidian. Then yellow road *(forking right at Oldwalls)* to Cheriton and Llanmadoc

PARKING At Brittania Inn *(meal or drinks afterwards)* or on official roadside park on right hand side just before reaching the inn MR447932. Parking in most of Llanmadoc and all of Cwm Ivy is restricted by yellow lines but there is a farm car park *(honesty box)* at the western end of Llanmadoc above Cwm Ivy.

LIFE SAVER - WHITEFORD LIGHTHOUSE

Wait for the tide it won't wait for you

WHERE TO START
THE car park at the Brittania Inn, Llanmadoc.

IN BLOOM - THE YELLOW IRIS

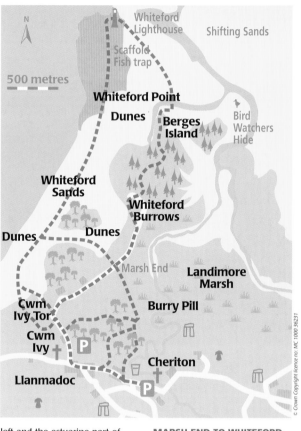

500 metres

Whiteford Lighthouse

Shifting Sands

Scaffold
Fish trap

Whiteford Point

Dunes
Berges Island

Bird Watchers Hide

Whiteford Sands

Whiteford Burrows

Dunes
Dunes
Dunes

Marsh End
Landimore Marsh

Cwm Ivy Tor

Burry Pill

Cwm Ivy

Cheriton

Llanmadoc

© Crown Copyright licence no: MC 1000 36231

LLANMADOC TO MARSH END

Walk uphill towards Llanmadoc village. Within less than 200 metres bear right up the old road between cottages.
At an opening on the right, a few metres further on turn right down a track towards a wooden gate. Go through this and steadily downhill towards Burry Pill, over a stile and past a picturesque white cottage on your left. Soon there is a second stile and an old quarry on the left conserved by the Glamorgan Naturalists Trust. This whole section is full of wild flowers in a number of habitats. Beyond the quarry go past a disused beehive-like pig stye and another quaint cottage called Pill House to reach the end of this track at a double stile with two dog slats in the middle.
(The left hand path goes off round the edge of Cwm Ivy Woods back to the middle part of Llanmadoc.)

The path leading from the right hand stile bears off to the right on to the tidal embankment leaving Cwm Ivy Marsh on your left and the estuarine part of Burry Pill on your right.

This easy walk provides many fine views of the estuary and over to Cwm Ivy Tor on your left and to North Hill Tor on your right.

At the end of the embankment at Marsh End *(unofficial name)* go through a kissing gate to join the alternative path which comes from the southwest through the woodland.
(By continuing straight on you can go over the dunes and see another profusion of wild flowers to reach the beach.)

MARSH END TO WHITEFORD LIGHTHOUSE

Note **Before starting on this section of the walk note the yellow warning sign about keeping on the track and avoiding any unexploded bombs.**

This was a bombing range during the Second World War but the chance of encountering a bomb is exceedingly rare since the majority were removed.

Turn right at the path crossroads and head on the four-wheel drive track in a northeasterly direction.

58

OUT AND ABOUT - A GRASS SNAKE

As you approach the pinewoods ahead of you avoid the temptation to bear away to the right along the edge of the estuary. Keep on the main track bearing to the left and then winding through the pinewoods and sand dunes.

Do not despair. After 500 metres or so you will come out on a clear dune area with a small area of the estuary on your left. *(This is not marked on most Ordnance Survey maps.)* You can head due north straight across this estuary at most states of the tide over the dunes towards Whiteford Point.

Your best route, however, is to continue on the path bearing around to the right. Once past the next clump of pine trees and well before reaching the birdwatchers' hide strike due north across the estuary arm *(this dries at about half tide).* Keep on the shingle beach and head northwest for the prominent sand dunes of Whiteford Point ahead of you.

Once at the point, if the conditions are not right you can return the same way or turn southwest and head all the way back along Whiteford Sands.

THE EXCURSION TO THE LIGHTHOUSE

Note **Before starting make sure the tidal conditions are right. Especially make sure that you do not attempt the last bit through the tide race around the lighthouse if the tide has turned. It comes in quickly and you could be stranded for eight to ten hours.**

From Whiteford Point, or thereabouts, head straight towards the clearly visible lighthouse *(if it is not visible do not go unless you are very confident with the compass).* You just have to make your own way zig-zagging along sand runnels and across rock pools. It all looks easy and it is, except for the last, deeper channel with fast flowing water right under the lighthouse. This dries only about one hour either side of low water.

THE LIGHTHOUSE TO THE BEACH ENTRANCE

Once you have enjoyed the aura and the isolation of this splendid monument to early Victorian engineering it will be time to turn back towards Whiteford Beach. You can linger long enough to enjoy it and watch the sea birds but always keep a weather eye on the tide.

The walk back across the rock pools and sandy patches should be enjoyed because all the time you can savour the ambience of the Loughor Estuary and the views across Carmarthen Bay. Once onto the beach it is a long slog to the entrance but you just have to keep going.

When you get further south you can deviate on to the dunes and wend your way back over them but you can get lost in these, especially if you are tired. Better to make the best of it and just keep going towards the beach entrance.

This usually becomes obvious by the marks of four-wheel drive vehicles and footprints. The beach track comes out at a gate and stile right under the northwestern tip of Cwm Ivy Tor.

EAGLE EYE - A HERON

PAST ITS BEST - AN OLD LIME KILN

THE BEACH ENTRANCE TO THE BRITTANIA INN

The walk back up to Cwm Ivy and through Llanmadoc to the Brittania Inn is easy. If you are tired, of course, you may find the slight inclines up into Cwm Ivy and Llanmadoc Rectory a little challenging. Do not despair, it will not be long before you are on the final easy and gentle walk through the village and down to the Brittania. Unless, of course, you choose to have a final fling on Cwm Ivy Tor before returning to the pub.

Cwm Ivy Tor is worth the diversion. It, and the delightful woodland walks from Cwm Ivy to Burry Pill estuary and back again to Llanmadoc village, can be the subject of a separate walk.

However, make the short sharp burst straight up the ridge of Cwm Ivy Tor and you will be rewarded with a feast of wild flowers in season and some brilliant views all over the Loughor Estuary and Whiteford Sands.

Make your way along the ridge with a stone wall on your right until you come to an obvious path descending in a zig-zag fashion down to the main beach track.

If you are avoiding the diversion up the tor and just wish to watch your friends toiling up the ridge, keep on going up the gravel road.

This leaves the craggy tor on your right and the wooded dunes on your left.

Once you reach some dwellings in the woodland on your left you pass a gate with the track going off to Marsh End. Now you are on tarmac and an incline up to Cwm Ivy hamlet.

Go through the kissing gate by the five-bar gate, then head steadily uphill past the church and rectory on your right into the village. From the Post Office, it is downhill to the Brittania.

WHAT TO LOOK FOR

Geology Llanmadoc Hill — formed of old red sandstone, earthworks known as The Bulwark, also Bronze Age cairns.

History Lime kiln and quarry on track past Burry Pill. Llanmadoc church and rectory. Church of St Madoc is said to have been founded in the 6th Century by the saint who was a pupil of St Cenydd's at Llangenydd College. The present church (possibly 13th Century) is the smallest in Gower.

Birds Shelduck, grey heron, egrets, curlew, oystercatcher, barnacle and Brent geese, many other wintering wildfowl. Green woodpecker, tits, nuthatch, treecreeper. Birdwatcher's hide overlooking Burry Pill and Loughor Estuary.

Conservation National Nature Reserve, great bird hide at Berges Island.

Visual aspect Great views of lighthouse, North Hill Tor, over to Llanelli and Pembrey.

Botany Flowers almost too plentiful to mention — iris, orchids, helleborine, sea aster, sea lavender, rosebay willowherb and large flowered evening primrose. Fungi such as the parasol mushroom, biting and yellow stonecrop.

Nautical interest Whiteford Lighthouse was built in 1842 and, for well over 100 years, was an essential beacon leading ships and fishing boats in and out of the Loughor Estuary. A shipwreck (mainly an engine block) remains at the north end of Whiteford Sands.

WAY IN - PAVILAND CAVE

DISTANCE	2.5 MILES/4KM
TIME	2 - 3 HOURS
GRADING	Mostly 3 but 4 - 5 in places

CAR Take A4118 from Swansea, then turn right on B4247 at Scurlage. Turn left down lane at Pitton MR 427877.

PARKING Park in the field at Pitton Farm −£1.50 charge in honesty box all year round. There is usually space.

OUTLINE An exciting and varied walk involving some easy paths over farmland, upper cliff paths and lower cliff scrambles. This is classified as a difficult walk because of several dangerous cliff overhangs and precipitous cliffs on the lower section. There are a number of splendid views of the headlands and of Worm's Head and lovely seascapes.

TRANSPORT

BUS Take the bus *(infrequent)* from Swansea Quadrant to Rhossili. Drop off at Pitton then walk down the lane to Pitton Farm

HOME SWEET HOME - KITTIWAKES ON THE CLIFFS

Walk on the wild side is not for the timid

WHERE TO START

The car park at Pitton Farm.

PITTON TO THE KNAVE

From the car park head south then south west first down then up the lane to Great Pitton Farm. Note the path *(signposted)* going off to the right to Thurba – this is the one you will return along on completion of your walk.

Keep going through two gates and then a third gate on a good farm track. Soon after the third gate you will come across another gate with a notice which clearly indicates that you turn right and head down towards the sea. At the bottom of the field go over a stile into a rocky area and head past a lime kiln on your right to the stile, which leads on to the upper coastal path.

At the path crossroads you can go straight down the dry slade of Ram Grove, straight to the sea. Our path goes off to the left, winding up and down over limestone rocks until it comes out in a rough scrub area above the slade. It soon reaches the cliff tops with their fine views and then turns south east to reach The Settlement – an ancient hill fort with a splendid commanding location MR 432864.

Now for the descent to The Knave. Ignore the more prominent inland path and, instead, go over the stile and set off downhill in a south-easterly direction. In a short time the distinctive knife edge slab of The Knave and the small islet of The Combs beyond will come into view.

Take great care going down towards the sea because on reaching the lower coastal path there is a sudden drop on the other side. Having studiously avoided this, turn left and look for a way down to the rocky gap between The Knave and the mainland.

(If you carry on the path without descending you will suddenly come to an abrupt end looking down into the western most of the deep fissures leading into Deborah's Bay – using the same name as the cave Deborah's Hole above the bay.)

THE ASSAULT OF THE KNAVE

This is definitely not for the faint-hearted. Take a good look at the ridge before you start. Your best way is straight up the western most ridge, keeping on the landward side when in any doubt – the drop is sheer on the seaward side. When you reach the top of the initial climb, edge your way along the ridge, again keeping on the landward side, until you reach the highest point.

Your reward will be great. This is one of the wilderness parts of Gower, visited by few people.

Here the world is your oyster. You can look down on to the

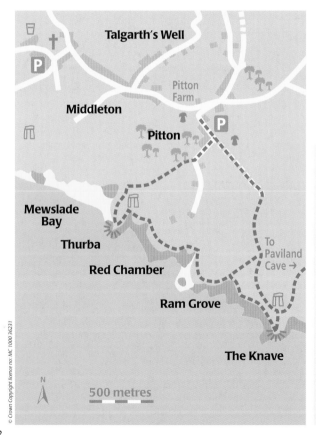

Talgarth's Well

Pitton Farm

Middleton

Pitton

Mewslade Bay

Thurba

Red Chamber

Ram Grove

To Paviland Cave →

The Knave

N

500 metres

ON THE ROCKS - RUGGED COASTLINE AT THE KNAVE, SOUTH GOWER

waves crashing into Deborah's Bay, see the archaic cormorants squabbling on The Combs or just look along the Magnificent Five Mile coast. Enjoy this while it lasts – always keeping a three-point hold on the rocks. It is not that difficult really – but then you have to get down. Best to edge back along the ridge then back slowly down the steeper part of the ridge.

Before leaving the limestone pavements to rejoin the main path enjoy the copious displays of sea lavender and golden samphire on the rocks.
Take note, once you have made it as far as The Settlement, it is not that far to the Paviland Cave, which can be reached by carrying on round the top coastal path instead of descending down to the Knave. This diversion will add another hour to your journey and is best done in company. The cave can only be reached at certain states of the low spring tides but at least if you cannot get to the cave you can see the blowhole at Fox Hole Slade.

THE KNAVE TO THURBA

Start on the limestone pavements at the bottom of The Knave. Head back up the path you have just come down until you reach the path coming down from The Settlement. Keep on going on the coastal path, remembering the overhang on your left. Go over a very rickety fence stile and on to a distinctive but narrow and rocky path. This will take you round the bottom of the limestone cliffs with a precarious drop to the left where, gradually, the path becomes more secure. Even now you will encounter precipitous overhangs from time to time so watch every step very carefully.

Eventually you will pick up an easy and safe track leading down to the pebble beach of Ram Grove. This is a good place to stop for refreshments and you can even take a swim with care. If you feel exhausted already you can go up the fairly easy gradient of the slade and return the way you came to Pitton Farm.

You are now well on your way to Thurba. The coastal path from now is nowhere near as difficult as before, although it is still not easy. Continue on the coastal path out from the bay. This leads on to a rough path past impressive castellated rocks, keeping well above the cliff edge until you reach a small spur with splendid views to the west. This is followed by a brief ledge which leads on to the path down into Red Chamber.

To get round this deep inlet go over another stile which is precariously close to an overhang and then past a second overhang before gaining the relative safety of a scree slope. Now the path becomes a little easier although if you want to escape at this stage you can take the brief climb out of Red Chamber to the stile above which is on the upper coastal path.

ALL AT SEA - BIRDS ON WATCH AT THE COMBS

Once round the deep fissure of Red Chamber keep going on the scree and steadily round the headland with a sphinx-like rock above you. Keep well above the indentations of Butter Slade and up and over another spur with a fine view now directly onto the eastern cliff of Thurba.

SET IN STONE - FOSSIL REMAINS

Just above another deep fissure you have a choice of three paths. The right hand one goes diagonally up to pick up the main path back to Pitton Farm. The middle path goes straight up to the top of Thurba Ridge close to a **Nature Conservancy Council sign asking walkers and climbers to keep clear of the outer edge during the bird breeding season from March 1 to April 10.** If it is out of season you can take the left hand path, keeping well clear of two more deep fissures on your left.

Cross over the fisherman's path but do not distract them for their concentration is even greater than that of golfers.

Now head up any one of the prominent limestone ledges which lead diagonally to the top. Be careful on reaching the top as a sheer rock face, much loved by climbers, awaits you on the other side.

Once on the top of the ridge you are onto another of Gower's rich wilderness areas — so close and yet so far from habitation. You can crawl or scramble right out to the tip but be wary of this whole ridge if there is a cross wind blowing.

THURBA TO PITTON

Now for the return home. Wherever you have reached, be it the outermost tip or the Nature Conservancy sign, make your way due north along the ridge. If you start from the tip you can peer over the Yellow Wall of the sheer cliffs on the western side. Enjoy the grandeur of the rocks and the sea birds flying but don't get carried away. All the time think of your safety and that of your companions.

Not too far up the ridge you will come across The Chimney, a deep funnel going straight down to the sea. You can safely go across the rock bridge on the seaward side of this but, if in any doubt, give it a wide berth. Soon you are up to the Nature Conservancy sign which will remind you that, to prevent disturbance to cliff nesting, there is a seasonal climbing restriction on the Yellow Wall and Thurba Head.

You are safe once you have reached the sign. Now head northeasterly over rocks and grassland to the stone wall corner where you join the upper coastal path. From now on it is an easy stroll, leaving the wall on your right.

As you enter the farm track there is a National Trust sign for Pen Thurba Point in the wall. Go through gates and stiles, through farm buildings until you reach the sign posts at Great Pitton Farm.

You have now rejoined the outgoing path. Turn left along the road and you will soon be in the car park.

WHAT TO LOOK FOR

Geology Paviland Cave may be reached at low tide. It is one of the most famous bone caves in Britain. 1823 saw the discovery of a headless skeleton called the Red Lady of Paviland because it was dyed with red ochre. The skeleton has now been found to be male and is at least 26,000 years old. More than 800 implement remains were also found, along with many animal remains. Above Paviland Cave is Yellow Top, a mass of limestone rock where an Iron Age promontory fort stands — a small settlement existed here 2,000 years ago.

Birds and other fauna Cormorants at The Combs. The Knave is a dramatic conical shaped rock which dominates the small inlet by Horse Cliff where seals can be spotted. Weasels, rabbits, birds of prey, fulmar, herring gull, kittiwakes, jackdaws, stonechat, yellowhammer, woodpecker, wagtail.

History and pre-history The Settlement, an ancient hill fort; Paviland Cave; Great Pitton Farm is one of the oldest farms on Gower and is heavily associated with smuggling and John Wesley — seperately that is.

Conservation National Trust.

Visual aspect Brilliant views along the south Gower coast all the way to Worm's Head.

Botany Sea lavender, golden samphire, common scurvy grass, sea thrift, gorse, orchid, harebell thistle.

DISTANCE	**3.4 MILES/5.5KM**
TIME	**2 HOURS**
GRADING	**2 but with one section of grade 4 on North Hill Tor**

OUTLINE This has a bit of everything — coastal wetlands, a mini-rock climb, fine views, a picturesque church, woodlands and two ancient pathways. One of the best coastal walks on Gower.

IN FLOWER - THE GREATER STITCHWORT

TRANSPORT

BUS Number 17 from Swansea Quadrant *(infrequent)* or Gower Explorer on Sundays and bank holidays in summer *(two per day)*.

CAR Take the B4295 from Gowerton or B4271 from Killay. Then take the yellow road at Llanrhidian and fork right for Llanmadoc at Old Walls. At Landimore village turn right and go through the village.

PARKING Unofficial car park at MR465935

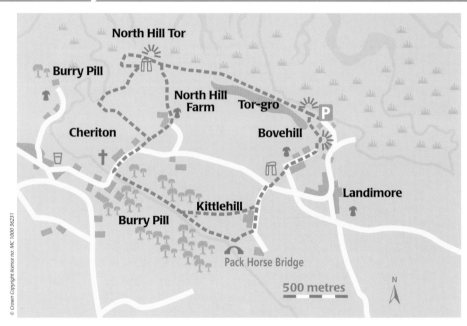

© Crown Copyright licence no: MC 1000 36231

North Hill Tor

Burry Pill

North Hill Farm   Tor-gro

Cheriton

Bovehill

Landimore

Kittlehill

Burry Pill

Pack Horse Bridge

500 metres

N

WHERE TO START

The gate with a National Trust sign: "Whiteford/ Landimore Marsh Conservation Area."

LANDIMORE TO NORTH HILL TOR

Go ahead in a slightly north of west direction on a rough stony four-wheel drive track. Leave the steep slopes of Tor-gro on your left and the mudflats on your right. You may see an old boat or two moored in one of many streamlets, and horses and ponies may come galloping towards you. A few lumps of sugar might reward their friendly interest. Some 1,000 metres or so from the gate a track goes steeply up to the left through the woods to North Hill Farm. Ignore

this and go on a littl further then turn south into Burry Pill estuary along a stone wall.

VISITORS - BUTTERFLIES

Now go over a wooden stile until you find an opening in the wall at MR 451938 where the

enclosed tidal flats drain into Burry Pill *(this part of the walk cannot be undertaken two hours either side of high water).*

From the opening walk across the flats in a westerly direction towards North Hill Tor.

Look for the hard ground and rough slope leading up to the north western spur of the Tor, leaving a large depression to your left.

This spur is a real rock scramble, which is slightly precarious in places.

The first pitch ends in a grassy slope, which opens into a small amphitheatre. There is no real path here but the scramble goes over to your right between the hawthorn trees then up the left-hand side of another mini ridge.

FLOURISHING - THE FOXGLOVE

At the top of this bear to the left and you are on top of North Hill Tor.

There are alternative routes from the tidal flats to the top of the tor. The best way is to look for an easy walk with a bit of rock scrambling to the south and east sides of the tor.

Once on top you have quite superb views all over the Loughor estuary to the north and east as far as the Black Mountains and to the Preseli Mountains and Pembrokeshire coast to the north and west. In the foreground you can see the full extent of the estuarine part of Burry Pill and in the middle ground you can look over to Cwm Ivy Tor, Llanmadoc Hill and Whiteford Point. This is a truly all round panoramic view. To the east of the tor there are extensive earthworks of an ancient settlement.

NORTH HILL TOR TO CHERITON

There are several routes south from the top of the tor down to the mud flats of Burry Pill.

Follow the sheep tracks down through the woodland until you reach the estuary.

Make your way along the edge of the mudflats until you reach the footpath sign and stile at the start of the path going up to North Hill Farm MR 450936.

This path now goes up a gentle slope over three stiles – recently restored by the Ramblers' Association – to reach the ancient track that goes from the main road to North Hill Tor.

Turn right here and go along the deeply incised track some 100 metres or so to the main road

At this stage, if you are feeling a little jaded you can take the road back towards Landimore.

However, you will be well rewarded and rejuvenated by going down into Cheriton village and taking the streamside walk to Kittlehill.

CHERITON AND PACKHORSE BRIDGE

As you go down into the village admire the small and ancient church of St Cadog on your right.

At this point turn left over the stone stile by the signpost *"Stembridge 2.35km"* and head along the edge of the field southwesterly towards the woodland.

Enter this over a stile then make your way on a well-defined path through the copse then over some clapboards *(slippery when wet)* to the open field.

You can strike diagonally uphill direct to Kittlehill Farm from here although the path is indistinct in places.

Much better to keep to the side of the field with woodland and Burry Pill stream to your right.

Go over four more stiles and reach the ancient green lane going up to Kittlehill.

Before going up the hill you really must turn to your right and go down to the ancient Packhorse Bridge.

This little bridge is quite different from everything else in Gower and quite a surprise.

It is so delightfully quiet and peaceful with its gently flowing stream. It is not so difficult to imagine the clip clop of horses and ponies in bygone years.

LANDMARK - NORTH HILL TOR

PACKHORSE BRIDGE TO LANDIMORE

Turn back from the bridge and head back up to the green lane over a stile towards Kittlehill.

The lane is quite deep and stony, and flanked by high stone walls.

Leave Kittlehill farm to your left then head along the lane to the main road. Cross the road with care, go over the stile and head in a northeasterly direction for Bovehill Farm.

Enter the farm by an old stone stile slightly to the right of the metal gate leading into the farmyard.

Continue past the farm buildings, and many barking dogs, to a metal gate at the far end of the settlement *(this gate is sometimes open)*. From here you may descend into Landimore village on your right or continue along the track past a white

cottage on your left *(more barking dogs)* to go down through woodland to regain the coastal track.

The third and best alternative is to take the very short climb onto the top of Bovehill Tor.

The view may not be quite as spectacular as North Hill Tor but it is very good none the less.

To descend from the tor if you want a little excitement go directly down the sharp spur ahead which is much easier to climb up than down.

If you are wise, and possibly slightly fatigued at this stage, you will look for an easy route onto the path and coastal path back to the car park.

WHAT TO LOOK FOR

Geology North Hill Tor, a prominent limestone headland overlooking marshes of Burry Estuary. Large earthwork site may date to Norman times. Landimore was once a small port which has traces of a small castle (also known as Bove Hill Castle) on the slopes of its westerly hill.

Botany Greater stitchwort, foxgloves, ferns such as the harts tongue fern, fungi, wood sorrel, wood anemone, bluebells, ramsons, snowdrops, celandines, common dog violet.
Many varieties of flower in limestone crags. Lichens, mosses

Birds and fauna Woodland rodents and many birds such as robins, blackbirds, tits, nuthatch, treecreeper, kestrel on North Hill Tor, jackdaws and rooks. Seabirds and wading birds in estuary. Many woodland butterflies.

Nautical interest Landimore — small port.

History 13th Century Cheriton Church, the Church of St Cadog. The churchyard was supposed to have been the sight of a fight between members of the Lucas family in 1770 but this story in highly suspect. Glebe House, next door, is 15th Century and is associated with the order of Knights Hospitallers of St John of the time of The Crusades. Ancient settlement on North Hill Tor.

Visual aspect Views from North Hill Tor and Bovehill Tor. Old mill stream on Burry Pill. Cheriton Church. Packhorse bridge and ancient green lanes.

NATURAL DRAMA - HUNTS BAY AND CLIFFS

DISTANCE	**2.5 MILES/4KM**
TIME	**2 HOURS, 3 if visiting the caves.**
GRADING	**2 on clifftop, 4 if on lower coastal path**

OUTLINE A nice easy clifftop walk with some fine views. The lower coastal walk is more difficult and quite dangerous in places. It is possible to get to the two caves, Mitchin Hole and Bacon Hole, from the clifftop without having to do the complete coastal walk.

TRANSPORT

BUS No 14, Swansea Quadrant to Pennard cliffs via Bishopston, every hour each way, Monday to Saturday

CAR by B4436 from Blackpill (Swansea Bay) to end of road at Pennard Cliffs.

PARKING In National Trust car park, fee for non-members.

RESIDENT BIRDLIFE - THE STONECHAT

Bacon Hole gives a taste for caving

THORNY PROBLEM - THE MUSK THISTLE

WHERE TO START
The National Trust car park in Pennard.

PENNARD TO HUNTS BAY — THE LOWER COASTAL WALK

Take the path straight down Fox Slade towards the sea. On reaching, the coastal path turn left. Then make your way as best you can along the path which is well worn in places but indistinct in others where the path is seriously overgrown with gorse. Continue on this path which leads to the rocks below. *You may divert here to reach Mitchin Hole Cave.* Now head along the coastal path around another series of crags until you come to another obstacle of impenetrable gorse bushes. Once again you have to divert upwards over crags and rocks. On this occasion, you will need to go right up to the cliff path

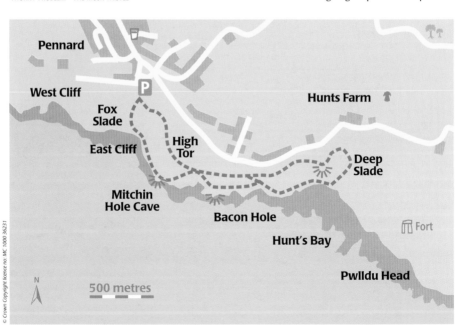

Pennard

West Cliff

Fox Slade

East Cliff

High Tor

Mitchin Hole Cave

Hunts Farm

Deep Slade

Bacon Hole

Hunt's Bay

Fort

Pwlldu Head

N

500 metres

© Crown Copyright licence no: MC 1000 3G231

CHANNEL VIEW - THE SUN SETS OVER THE BRISTOL CHANNEL

above. You have no alternative here for any attempt to get through the gorse will prove impossible although it may be cleared on some future occasion.

Once on the clifftop, walk for a very short distance before taking the prominent path diagonally all the way down to the sea. This leads safely down to Bacon Hole another prehistoric site. Once the cave has been visited and you have made your way back to the lower coastal path, the rest of the walk is easy. First of all, you will need to negotiate a series of sloping rock slabs before getting on to a well-worn path.

Once you are in Deep Slade, head straight up the valley until you see a prominent path heading off to your left. Go straight up this short, steep slope to reach the road above.

It will be seen from this description of the lower coastal walk that *anyone who has any doubt about this should stick to the clifftop walk*. The one lower path which is relatively safe and easy is the one direct from the cliff top to Bacon Hole.

BRANCH LINE - SPECKLED WOOD BUTTLERFLY

HUNTS BAY TO PENNARD CLIFFS — A CLIFFTOP WALK

At the roadside look for the path, which leads off almost immediately away from but roughly parallel to the road. Keep on this path until it gradually diverts away from the road and takes you to your first

able to advise them about its delights and dangers.

If you should meet one of the birdwatching experts, they in turn will be able to inform you about the interesting bird life — this is one of the few places on Gower where choughs may be sighted.

WASHED OUT - SEASPRAY ON PEBBLES

headland. This will give you a view straight down to the rock slabs and Bacon Hole below. You can, if you wish, return to Pennard Cliffs the easy way along the road. You can also take one of a number of tracks which keep more directly in between the road and the clifftop.

Far better is to take each little headland in turn and enjoy the different views that they open up. Since these are quite popular paths, you will surely wish to pass the time of day with fellow walkers. If you have been on the coastal path, you may be

The most prominent part of the clifftop walk is High Tor with some suggestion here of earthworks or mineral workings.

This site has particularly good views to the east to Pwlldu Head and to the west down into Fox Slade but also all the way across to Oxwich Bay. A nice easy undulating walk will take you back to the car park.

WHAT TO LOOK FOR

Geology Hunts Bay has extensive limestone pavements exposed at low water.

Hunts Bay to the west of Pwlldu Head, named after the land and farm above Deep Slade which William le Breos presented to his huntsman, William de Hunde.

History, prehistory, caves Iron Age promontory fort on Pwlldu Head; Mitchin Hole — largest of the coastal caves — extensively excavated, remains of bison, hyena and elephant; traces of human occupation; Bacon Hole — name comes from red oxide streaks on cave wall, evidence of human occupation in Iron Age, Roman and more recent times, prehistoric animal remains.

Conservation National Trust land.

Birds Stonechats, wheatears, herring gulls, curlew, plover, oystercatcher, choughs, green woodpecker.

Botany Kidney vetch, sea thrift, thistles, gorse, orchids, vetch, common scurvy and viper's bugloss

THRIVING - GORSE

Visual Aspect Great views over to Devon on a clear day, shipping in the bay.

On the rocks

- Gower is made up of a series of sedimentary deposits of the Carboniferous and Devonian eras, all between 200 and 400 million years old.

- These deposits range from the newest coal measures through the millstone grit and carboniferous limestone to the oldest red sandstone rocks of the Devonian era.

- These sedimentary rocks have been subjected to massive earth movements and folded into a series of synclines (folding downwards) and anticlines (folding upwards). The hard rocks of the old red sandstone have resisted erosion more so they form the highest peaks of Cefn Bryn, Rhossili Down, Llanmadoc Hill and Ryer's Down.

- In contrast, the weaker rocks of the millstone grit have been eroded away to form valleys at Oxwich Bay and Port Eynon.

- In between and prominent in most of the coastal areas are the massive layers of carboniferous limestone made up of minute sea creatures.

- During the recent ice ages, there was no glaciation on Gower. However, there are a number of examples of glacial drift and boulder clay on top of the base rocks.

- In addition, the Dunvant Gap (where the path/cycle track on the old railway line passes) was once an outfall of a large glacial lake.

- The changes in sea level during the ice ages resulted in several raised beaches, best seen on the south coast.

- The long beaches at Rhossili and Oxwich Bay are excellent examples of contemporary beach formation in action.

WHERE THE LAND MEETS THE SEA - CLIFFS AT THE BASE OF PAVILAND CAVE, SOUTH GOWER

- Likewise, the formation of sand dunes at Whiteford Point, Oxwich Bay, Nicholaston Burrow, Penmaen and Pennard Burrows, are examples of contemporary action including the 15th and 16th Century smothering of villages around Three Cliffs Bay.

- This is only a brief comment on geology and physical geography but it gives a glimpse of Gower's geological delights.

- There is little doubt that the peninsula of Gower is a geologist's treat.

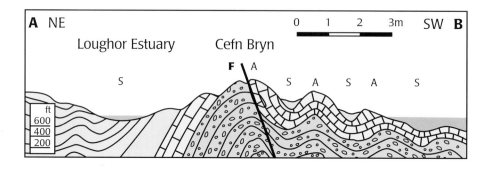

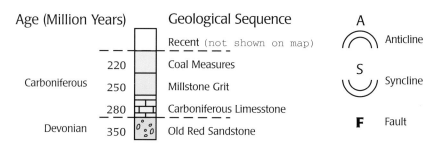

Age (Million Years)	Geological Sequence	
	Recent (not shown on map)	
220	Coal Measures	
Carboniferous		
250	Millstone Grit	
280	Carboniferous Limesstone	
Devonian 350	Old Red Sandstone	

A Anticline

S Syncline

F Fault

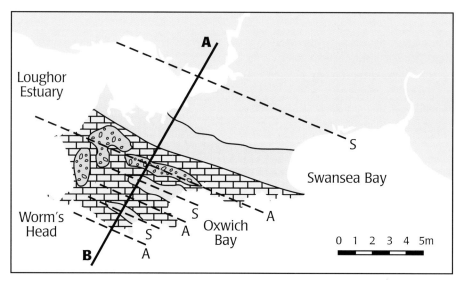

Geological cross section and map adapted from "The Natural History of Gower" by Mary Gillham (after T.R.Owen) with permission of the publishers D Brown & Sons Ltd Cowbridge.

Monthly variation in tides

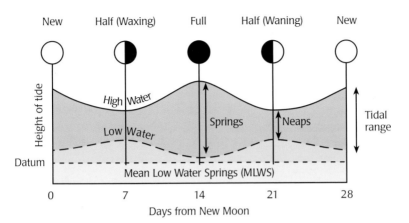

New   Half (Waxing)   Full   Half (Waning)   New

Height of tide

High Water

Low Water

Springs   Neaps

Tidal range

Datum

Mean Low Water Springs (MLWS)

0   7   14   21   28

Days from New Moon

THE TIDES

- A knowledge of the tides is of interest to the Gower walker. It will allow you to know when to reach islands and cross bays.

- The tides of the Bristol Channel have a high range, the highest spring tides occurring twice a month at full moon and new moon. The lower, neap tides occur twice a month at half moon. There are two high tides and two low tides every day.

- The spring tides of Swansea Bay and Gower tend to have high water in the early morning and late afternoon. The neap tide highs occur a little after midday and midnight.

- Tide tables may be bought from some shops. The times of high water are published daily in the Evening Post.

GEOGRAPHICAL TERMS

Slade A narrow dry gully or valley leading down to the sea, eg Mewslade.

Tor A small, exposed limestone pinnacle or peak, eg North Hill Tor, Great Tor.

Burrows A series of hillocks and depressions, mainly sand dunes, eg Penmaen Burrows.

Pill Small stream, eg Nicholaston Pill

Holm Island, eg Burry Holms of Norse origin.

From the earliest time of man's habitation of the British Isles there has been evidence of activity on Gower.

Caves at Mitchin Hole, Bacon Hole and at Paviland have given some indication of man's occupation of the peninsula at the time of the hairy mammoth and other prehistoric animals.

Archaeologists' excavations have revealed several settlements and fortifications which may have been occupied by the ancient Celtic Silures tribe at least 2,000 years ago. Such sites may be seen at Rhossili, Burry Holms, Thurba, North Hill Tor and Penmaen Burrows.

The ancient field system, The Vile, at Rhossili, is another example of early settlement.

In this case, the long thin strips were each one-and-a-half acres and crop rotation kept the land fertile.

Life could never have been peaceful for any length of time anywhere on Gower and there were many tribal conflicts as well as invasions by the Romans and English.

The first outside invasion of note was that of the Vikings in the ninth and 10th Centuries.

They spread all along the coasts of the Irish Sea. They may have left few artefacts or hoards as in eastern England but they did leave a number of place names. Swansea — Sweyne's Eye or island — is one. Holms — also island — is another, and Staffal Haegr on the Loughor Estuary must be another. The Worm's Head — the wurm being a Viking serpent/dragon — is another.

It was in the early part of the second millennium that the castles sprang up and the churches became established.

THE LANGUAGE

Meanings of Welsh words used regularly in Gower place names

Pwll	pool
Ddu	black
Llan	church, parish, village
Coed	wood
Cwm	valley
Pen	headland, point
Maen	field, rock
Cefn	stony outcrop, ridge
Bryn	hill, beautiful view
Rhos	moorland
Allt	hillside
Yr	of (the)
Clawdd	ditch, bank, dyke

Welsh names are more likely to be found in north Gower than in south Gower which has been more influenced by Norse, English and Cornish words.

The castles were set up by the English landlords to repel the Celtic tribes and, later, in an attempt to repel the Normans. Their legacies have been left in varying states of repair at Oystermouth, Pennard, Oxwich and Weobley. These are not the only castles but they are the ones most obvious to the coastal walker.

Moving on to more recent times there is a good deal of physical and written evidence of man's quarries at Rhossili, Oxwich Bay and Pwlldu — these are all indications of a flourishing limestone industry.

The stone was regularly shipped to Devon for agricultural purposes and to Swansea for the town's then flourishing copper industry. Much local use was also made of the limestone as seen by the many limekilns that can be seen on coastal walks.

The need for ships to transport goods resulted in the setting up of lighthouses at Mumbles Head and Whiteford Point and a lightship on the Helwick Sands off Worm's Head. In spite of these navigational aids, numerous wrecks may be found all around the coast. The most famous of all and clearly visible is that of the Helvetia, wrecked on Rhossili Beach in 1887. Perhaps less well known and marked by a buoy just off Port Eynon Head is the pleasure steamer Ivanhoe accessible only to skilled divers.

Shipwrecks, in turn, led to the need for lifeboat stations at Mumbles Head and Horton and a breeches buoy station at Rhossili. The sad loss of life of some of these heroic lifeboat men is commemorated in Oystermouth and Port Eynon churches.

BEACON - KING ARTHUR'S STONE, ON CEFN BRYN

At Rhossili Church is a memorial plaque to another nautical hero, Petty Officer Edgar Evans, of Scott of the Antarctic fame. Born in the Gower community of Middleton, he went on to become part of Scott's ill-fated expedition to the South Pole in 1911-12.

This is but a glimpse of some of the fascinating history of Gower. We should also note the many stories told by the famous Rev JD Davies, rector of Llanmadoc. He told of trips by horse and trap across the Loughor Estuary, of rescues from shipwrecks and of much smuggling. One only has to go to Pwlldu on a dark night to imagine the boats unloading wine casks.

Then what about the Salt House at Port Eynon and the mysteries of nearby Culver Hole with its pigeon lofts? If the experts cannot provide us with all the answers, there is room still for amateur archaeologists or historians to provide us with some more.

One other historical item of note is the network of old trade routes or farm tracks. Some tracks are included in the coastal walks described here. There is, for example, the green lane that goes over the packhorse bridge on Burry Pill. There are several old lanes around Leasons, near Weobley Castle, and there is an ancient track from Pwlldu to Pennard Church. We should not forget the railway buff either. Gower has had its share of railways. There is the much-lamented Mumbles Railway — thought to be the first passenger railway in the world. Then there is the old LMS line from Blackpill to Gowerton now a popular walking and cycling track. The north coast also had its line, all the way from Gowerton via Penclawdd to Crofty. This too is being developed as a cycle/walkway.

Little has been said about the folklore — for the walker this is not as tangible as the history but it is worth thinking about. Add to that the adventures of the great Swansea poet Dylan Thomas and you have more than enough for a fireside chat. This is something for a quiet drink in the local pub after a long walk. Enjoy!

Take care walking - some hints

- Most of the walks in this guide involve easy, regular tracks. Some cover more difficult off-main track scrambles and climbs.

- Sometimes these are nothing more than sheep tracks. The walks also involve, from time to time, steep rock climbs as on the cliffs of Three Cliffs Bay, or scary cliff walks with dramatic overhangs.

- On many of the walks there are the most spectacular sea views with ever-changing cloud and seascapes. These are a sheer joy which can still be captured on the more regular paths, but for the slightly more adventurous they can be a revelation and an experience not to be missed.

- None of these walks is inherently dangerous as long as normal precautions are observed.

- Wear good boots and waterproof/windproof clothing, especially in winter.

- Carry a survival kit and take plenty of food and fluid. Keep fit and beware of fatigue.

- Take extra gear if you wish, such as cameras and binoculars, but remember that these add weight and, for some of these walks, flexibility and lightness is the order of the day.

- These walks can be undertaken by less experienced walkers if accompanied by a more experienced one. Ideally they should be taken in company but the lone walker will get great joy out of these too.

- Some of the walks are not for children under 10 because of the "scare factor" and the need to avoid panic.

- It is important to observe the need for conservation of the land, the flora and fauna.

- Great care should be taken at all times to avoid trespass on private land unless there are recognised paths across it – remember, farmland is private.

- Some of the rights of way on private land on Gower remain contentious. They will only be resolved in time when the Countryside and Rights of Way Act (CROW) 2000 is fully implemented and individual cases are resolved by agreement or tested in a court of law.

Safety

If you are walking over difficult or remote terrain and especially if you are alone, always carry a survival kit. Even on the easy paths there is always the possibility of tripping or falling.

Be particularly careful in wet and windy conditions. Stick to the paths but if you do deviate and do some rock scrambling make sure you keep well within your own limits of competence, endurance and physical fitness.

Keep within your own "scariness factor" or "comfort zone". Always make sure that an escape route is available.

Never stint on good quality, waterproof, breathable boots like Brasher Hill-Masters, and waterproof and windproof clothing. Good names with breathable fabric like Gortex are strongly recommended.

A compass is useful as sea mists can come down on some coastal walks and you can get lost in dunes.

If you sustain an injury or illness which immobilises you, you will need to work out your tactics depending on whether or not you have company.

If the party is three or more there is no problem. One works out where to locate the nearest help (farm or road) and makes straight for it. The other stays with the injured person.

If there are only two in the party there is more of a problem. Do you stay or do you go for help?

This really depends on the circumstances and can

SURVIVAL KIT

Basics Small torch & spare batteries, compass, whistle, knife, waterproof matches, survival bag (aluminium foil)

Fluids Water, energy drink, fruit drink, hot soup, tea or coffee

Food Chocolate, biscuits, muesli bars, flapjack bars, nuts, dried fruit, mint cake (keep these in a sealed waterproof bag in a rucksack, bumbag or anorak pocket)

First aid Plaster, scissors, anti-histamine cream, blister protection, asprin or paracetamol, sun cream (factor 15)

Clothing Spare lightweight clothing (shirt or sweater), woolly hat/balaclava (sun hat in summer), gloves/mittens, waterproof and windproof Gortex anorak and trousers

Good map of locality

only be decided on the spot. As a general rule, if the casualty is reasonably comfortable and safe it is better to go for help.

If you are on your own or your companion has stayed with you then you must try to attract attention. Do this by shouting help at regular intervals.

If alone or with children **carry a mobile phone** but remember there are many blind spots especially in slades and below cliffs.

As an alternative, sound the international distress signal of six short whistle blasts or flashes of a light or mirror every minute in the same way.

Instead of this you may use the Morse Code SOS sign which is three dots, three dashes and three dots.

While doing this look for secure shelter and do everything possible to conserve warmth, food and fluid.

The solo walker should always leave information with someone about his/her likely route and time of return.

If they have not returned within a designated number of hours of the expected time the emergency services should be alerted.

BIBLIOGRAPHY

Davies. Rev. J D
History of West Gower (4 volumes)
1877 to 1898

Davies. James A
Dylan Thomas's Swansea, Gower and Laugharne -
A Pocket Guide
Cardiff University of Wales
Press/The Western Mail 2000

Davies. Paul R
Historic Gower
C Davies 1997

Douglas-Jones. Peter R
Three Corners of Gower Photographs
Port Talbot D W Jones Printers 1997

Gillham. Mary E
The Natural History of Gower
Cowbridge. D Brown and Sons 1977 (reprinted 1983)

Green. Amanda
Family walks in Gower
Cromford Scarthin Books 1993

Morris. Bernard (editor)
Gower The Gower Society Swansea 1995

National Trust
The Gower Peninsula
The National Trust 1991

Neville. George T
British Regional Geology - South Wales
London HMSO 1937 (third edition 1970)

Ridge. Ruth
Gower Walks
Swansea The Gower Society 1991 (reprinted 1994)

Strawbridge. D and Thomas. P J (editors)
A Guide to Gower
Swansea The Gower Society (new and revised edition) 1999

Vaughan Thomas. Wynford
Portrait of Gower
Robert Hale 1976 (second edition 1987)

West Glamorgan Ramblers Association
Walking around Gower
Swansea South Wales Evening Post 1991 Second (revised) edition 1993

Williams. Dianne M
Cadw Guidebook: Gower
Cardiff CADW Welsh Historic Monuments 1998

Wilson. Lois
Wildflowers in their seasons
Cowbridge. D Brown and Sons undated

MAPS

Ordnance Survey (Explorer 10)
Gower 1:25000
Southampton Ordnance Survey

Ordnance Survey (Landranger Series No 159) Swansea, Gower & surrounding area 1:50000
Southampton Ordnance Survey

USEFUL CONTACTS

Bishops Wood Nature Reserve/Countryside Centre
Tel 01792 361703

British Trust for Ornithology (BTO)
Tel 01792 405363

British Trust for Conservation Volunteers (BTCV)
The Environment Centre
Swansea SA1 1RY
Tel 01792 456224

Bus Services - First Cymru
Quadrant Bus Station, Swansea
Tel 01792 580580 / 582233

CADW Welsh Historic Monuments
Cardiff CF10 3NQ
www.cadw.wales.gov.uk
Tel 02920 500200

Countryside Council for Wales
Tel 01792 763500/390320

Countryside Services
Planning Dept Swansea City & County, Swansea
Tel 01792 635094

Glamorgan Wildlife Trust
(Naturalist's Trust)
Tel 01656 724100 / 367881

Gower Ornithological Society
Tel 01639 751020

Gower Heritage Centre
Parkmill Swansea
Tel 01792 371206

The Gower Society
Swansea Museum, Victoria Road, Swansea SA1 1SN
Tel 01792 753763

National Trust
Gower Office, Reynoldston
Tel 01792 390636

National Trust Shop & Visitor Centre
Rhossili Gower (open daily mid Mar - end Oct, all weekends and Wed - Sun Nov - Dec)
Tel 01792 390707
www.nationaltrust.org.uk

Ramblers Association
Welsh Office, Wrexham
Tel 01978 855148
www.ramblers.org.uk

Royal Society for Protection of Birds (RSPB)
Tel 01792 842927
Welsh Office Newtown Powys
SY16 2AB
Tel 01686 626678

Tourism South and West Wales, Swansea
Tel 01792 281212

Tourist Information Centres
Llanelli Tel 01554 772020
Mumbles (Oystermouth Square)
Tel 01792 361302
Swansea (near Quadrant Bus Station) Tel 01792 468321

Wales Tourist Board, Cardiff
Tel 029 2049 9909

Wildfowl and Wetlands Trust
Llwynhendy
Llanelli
Tel 01554 741087